Fearless Mujer,

You Were Created for **MORE**

A JOURNEY TO HEALING, LETTING GO, AND FINDING PURPOSE

7-2022

Natalie,
thanks for helping me
during my time in BAIB.
You're a blessing and an amazing
person.
           Love You.
                ♡ Micaela

MICAELA DEEGAN

P.S.
Natalie is
my daughter's
name ♡

Dear Fearless Mujer, You Were Created for More

Trilogy Christian Publishers
A Wholly Owned Subsidary of Trinity Broadcasting Network
2442 Michelle Drive, Tustin, CA 92780

Manufactured in the United States of America
10 9 8 7 6 5 4 3 2 1
Library of Congress Cataloging-in-Publication Data is available.

ISBN 978-1-68556-631-9
ISBN 978-1-68556-632-6 (ebook)

Dedication

This book is dedicated to my daughter, the bravest girl I've ever known. You inspire me more than you could ever know. Your light and joy can fill a whole room. Thank you for teaching me what courage truly means. You are loved more than you could ever know.

I would also like to dedicate this book to the women who have ever wondered if their life truly mattered: The ones who had to fight to survive. The women who have had their voices silenced, you matter, and your voice is powerful.

Acknowledgements

To my husband, thank you for always believing in me. Thank you for loving me in my darkest moments. Our marriage has been far from perfect, but I have no doubt that God aligned our paths. You never criticize my big ideas or the big dreams that God puts in my heart. You have loved me for exactly who I am.

To the women who read this book before it was an actual book, thank you for keeping it top secret. Alexis Cano, Shirley Giraldo, Anel Aguirre-Cervantes, and Clairessa Cruz, thank you for your willingness to read it. I appreciate each of you more than you could ever know.

To the women who have seen my book journey, thank you so much for celebrating me.

Table of Contents

Introduction

My eight-year-old daughter whispered words in my ear that no mother should ever have to hear. With tears in her eyes, she let out a secret that she had been keeping for some time. She finally found the courage within her eight-year-old heart and soul to let her secret out. *She was being molested.*

I felt so nauseated and weak. The words she shared with me were enough to make me curse and throw my fish sticks on the floor. I tried to stay calm, but I was all over the place. Finally, my husband and I managed to calm our daughter down. I knew that I had to share this with my dad. It was his brother who was doing this to her. After age eleven, I lived with my dad because of my parents' divorce. He pretty much taught me everything I knew. I wouldn't say that he was my hero, but he was the parent who I felt kind of got me. I had a special bond with him and went to him for pretty much anything. So, of course, I had to share this with him because I needed my dad at that moment.

Our conversation did not go the way I would have hoped, and I was so disappointed. Despite that, I knew what I had to do. After leaving the police station, my family and I stopped to put gas in the car. I remember telling myself that I would probably never speak to my dad again.

I never expected to hear my daughter say something like what she shared with me that day. She had been experiencing something that no innocent child should ever have to experience. I knew that I had to be her voice. I knew that I had to protect her like no one ever did for me. I had to teach her that strong women stand up, speak up, and slay whatever comes to attack them. But you see, using your voice will cost you sometimes. Speaking up will remove people from your life but slaying what comes against you will make you fearless.

You might think that the story was over after that. I could see how you would get that impression, but it was the exact opposite. Yes, this part of my life was painful. I felt pain like never before. Have you ever been in a situation that is so painful you feel like you can't even breathe? Let's just say that I had to take intense deep breaths for a really long time. I had to learn to put all my faith in God. I had to learn that I had to let go of everything that I knew if I was ever going to be okay. It didn't happen overnight. It took many painful nights of crying out to God and asking, "Why?" I couldn't understand why someone who loved me would turn their back on me.

I remember waking up in the middle of the night and asking God why someone would want to hurt my daughter and just asking what any person would ask, "Why?" As I cried, I opened my Bible and read a verse I had never read before, "Listen, O daughter, consider and give ear; forget your people and your father's house" (Psalm 45:10). I don't think it could be any clearer. I had to let go of what I had known my whole life. Maybe you have never read the Bible, and I get that. But you should know that, although the Bible was written ages ago and for a different group of people, God still uses those very words to speak to us and encourage us. I knew that night that if I was going to be okay, I had to let go of everything I knew and someone that I had loved my whole life. I knew that I had to put all my trust in God. Maybe you don't believe in all that God stuff, and I respect that. But you see, I have to be honest with you and tell you this, God used a painful part of my life to guide me into learning who I really was and that I had authority.

That's why I wrote this book. I wrote it for you because I want to help guide you on a journey of learning who you really are and how to step into your authority. You see, sometimes we go through really devastating situations that seem impossible to overcome. Sometimes we hold on to our past mistakes and what people have said about us, which causes us to live in fear. Have you ever felt fear? The kind that says you are not good enough, smart enough, or pretty enough? Have you replayed the voices of others over and over in your head? Have you felt like no one really gets you? Have you lived with the criticism of your family? Have you believed things about yourself and life in general because that's what your parents taught you? If you have answered yes, to even one of these questions, please stick around. This book will challenge you to see yourself from a different perspective. Why? Because to become a fearless *Mujer*, you must be willing to see yourself in a whole new light. I know you're reading this book because you are already a strong *Mujer*. You're ready to do what is necessary to empower yourself. I want you to be that girl that follows her dreams and lives them. I know that you know there is more for your life, and girl, I am cheering for you!

Amiga, please make yourself comfortable, grab your *cafecito* or glass of wine. We are about to dive into a journey of discovering who you are so that you can begin stepping into your authority. So, are you ready? Let's do this.

The Healing Journey

Have you ever heard the saying *time will heal*? I have no idea who said that but let me give them credit. Let me also tell you something. I have no idea what that means! I wouldn't say that time heals. I would say that with time it gets better. You learn to adjust, breathe new air, and see things differently. I would say that with time, letting go gets more manageable.

Let me ask you this: were you devastated when you broke up with someone? Was it hard when you got divorced? Was it easy for you? It probably was devastating, challenging, and not easy. But you learned to let go, right? That's because we begin to adjust to our new way of life, including letting go of people. You see, humans were created with an incredible survival instinct. We can learn to overcome a lot if we dare to allow ourselves to be uncomfortable. The problem is that we don't always like change. I have never met anyone who ever told me, "I love being uncomfortable," or, "I love when things dramatically change in my life." That's because no one likes to go through hard things. Sometimes we go through things in life that are like a real-life *telenovela*. We go through things that crush us and push us down.

Back in the day, before I ever went on my faith walk, girl, I used to feel like life had dragged me by the hair and used me as a mop to clean the floor. I felt so beat up by life and by this world.

Life will do that to you sometimes, but not everyone is brave enough to talk about that. Most people would rather shove down all the ugly parts of their lives and pretend it never happened. Have you ever seen someone post a picture on social media and say, "Hey, look at this time life punched me in the stomach."? I haven't seen anything like that. But I've seen pictures of people saying, "Hey, look at when my life was all jacked up, and God did something with it." I love those kinds of posts, and if you haven't seen one like that, find one because it will inspire you.

I firmly believe God does incredible things in the lives of people. Sometimes, this will require you to let go of what you knew or who you knew because they are a stumbling block to where God intends you to be. You see, there is something so great inside of you. You are here because there is a greater purpose for you and your life. You are not here by accident. God purposefully put you here for this time. Let that sink in for a minute.

You might be thinking, "Girl, if you only knew my life," or "no, that's not me," or "my life has been so crazy, and I've messed up so much." I get that. All those thoughts and similar ones used to replay in my mind. I believed every word I spoke over myself. But I have learned that I have to challenge my beliefs about who I am, my capabilities, and how my life should be. I have learned that my life is not meant to stay stuck, and neither is yours. Your life is meant to be something beautiful, and it doesn't matter who thinks otherwise. Maybe you were told that you would never be anyone in this life. It might be that you were told that you were worthless or that no one loved you or liked you. Whatever it was for you, it's time to let go of the words spoken over you. In the next chapter, we will dive into rewriting some of these lies, but for now, I want to ask you two questions. If you can't answer them right now, it's okay. If the questions are too hard for you, that's okay too. Just imagine that I'm sitting at your kitchen table or on the couch with you, and for a second, I'll hold your hand and help you answer these questions. Here it goes.

Would you be willing to confront some of your pain so that you could heal? Would you be ready to heal if you knew it meant you would step into your authority? Part of stepping into your authority and becoming fearless means that you will have to learn to heal. You will have to go through a healing journey, and the truth is that healing hurts like crazy. Not all people are willing to heal because it's uncomfortable, challenging, and painful.

To heal, you have to confront your pain, rip some band-aids off, and clean the wound. You will have to face old wounds, some of which you weren't even aware were there. The healing process hurts, and you will feel fear rise up inside you when you decide you are ready to confront the pain. But fear isn't what you think it is. Fear is kind of tricky. It makes you believe you are in danger, but you're just uncomfortable. When you choose to embark on a healing journey, you are stepping out of your comfort zone. If you have never stepped out of your comfort zone, you will feel nervous and afraid. It may also shock you. But just know that you can overcome the fear. You are the boss of yourself, not your fear.

Don't let fear hold you captive or paralyze you. Take baby steps if you need to, but don't let fear stop you. Don't allow fear to call the shots in your life because I'm telling you right now, if you let fear call the shots in your life, it will never stop. It will own you, control you, and never let you go. Remember that fear is just a survival instinct. Fear is what tells us when we are in danger. Sometimes, it can be helpful, like when you're by yourself at the store, and see a creepy person in the parking lot. But it's not that helpful when you're trying to do something good for yourself, like stepping out in faith so that you can heal. Remember that it's vital that you don't skip the healing process on your way to becoming a fearless *Mujer*.

Can I be honest with you? You know your girl over here is not a therapist, right? I'm not a therapist or a psychologist, but I like to think that I have a Ph.D. in overcoming pain and setbacks in my own life. I believe that education is extremely important, and when I have the honor of meeting an educated *Mujer*, it inspires me. But, do you know what inspires me even more? I'm inspired when I hear stories of women who had everything against them and slain all that was meant to break them. Women who get back up after life has bruised and battered them are truly powerful women. Those are the women that you don't mess with! But you know what makes those women even better? The women who heal when life should have destroyed them become unstoppable! They find the freedom to be who they were created to be without worrying about what anyone thinks.

How often have you tried to pursue something you were excited or passionate about, only to have someone tell you your idea was too crazy? I experienced this when someone explained that I had to let go of my dreams because I was a mom. This person was older than I was at the time, and I thought they had all the answers. When you're in your early twenties, you think older people have it all figured out. That's what I used to believe, mostly because I wasn't secure in who I was.

Learning to heal reveals so much about yourself. You will have to be uncomfortable and comfortable with yourself all at the same time. That might not make sense right now, but if you've been through your own healing journey, you get me. I want you to know that this part of stepping into your fearlessness is going to hurt. Confronting your hurt hurts. It's not for the weak.

Before I continue, I want to be completely honest with you. I'm not here to trigger you. I mentioned to you that I am not a therapist. If you struggle with depression or feel triggered at any point during the first chapter, please let your therapist know you will be reading this. Maybe you can also take your time reading this chapter. If you are reading this and you're like, "Micaela, I'm good in the healing area," please feel free to read ahead. I don't like to sugarcoat anything, so I have to be honest with you, and if you're reading this book, I can imagine that you want someone to keep it real with you. You see, a lot of women want to feel empowered. So, they listen to the podcasts and watch the motivational speakers. They feel empowered for a few weeks or months, but then something might happen, or someone might say something, and the motivation high is gone. It becomes a feeling rather than something that has transformed their heart.

So, although my passion is to inspire and empower you to be a fearless *Mujer*, we cannot take a shortcut. Short cuts will cost you more than you could ever know, and because you only have one life and one shot to leave your legacy and to make your mark in this world, there can be no shortcuts. So, if you were hoping to find a book telling you an easy way to step into your fearlessness,

I am so sorry. This is not that book. This book is for the woman ready to do the hard work of *heart work* because she is willing to become who she was created to be.

The truth is, there are so many women walking around with band-aids covering their wounds. They might look put together on the outside, but they are covered in band-aids on the inside, and if anyone dares rip them off, they run. How do I know this? That was me until God came along and ripped off my band-aids and made me confront my wounds, and let me tell you, it was painful. I had a band-aid on top of a band-aid, and my wounds couldn't heal. I'm not here to take your band-aids off. I'm here to show you how to take them off for yourself.

Part of becoming an empowered woman is learning to empower yourself. Once you can do that, it's so powerful. Confronting your pain and learning to heal will make you unstoppable. And it won't just make you powerful and unstoppable. You will teach the next generation of women how to confront their pain. I don't know about you, but I want my daughter to be a better version of me. I want her to know who she is so it doesn't faze her when someone tries to tell her she is someone other than who she really is. I want her to be so empowered that fear is like a cute baby to her. I don't want my daughter walking around covered in band-aids, and I don't think you want yours to walk around that way either. We have to raise the next generation of women to be secure in who they are. When challenging circumstances arise, or people try to tell them they're someone other than who they are, they will continue to walk in confidence because they already know who they are. You have been entrusted with the next generation of *Mujeres*, and that's another reason why you must be brave enough to start your healing journey.

I never expected what happened with my daughter to happen. I never expected that I would have to let go of my dad. I was devastated, and I couldn't see past that moment. I was a girl on a journey, and my journey seemed hopeless. Honestly, if I didn't have my faith, I probably would have self-sabotaged. I probably would have taken shots of tequila every night. I'm just being honest with you. I am so grateful I had my faith to hold on to. But back in the day before my walk with God, girl, that would've been me. I have told women who listen to my podcast that it's because of God if they even like me a little. So, I'm not going to sit here and say that I had it all figured out after this traumatic event happened in my life because the truth is I didn't.

At that time, I was working for a cosmetology school at the corporate office in the student services department. I was in charge of calling students who weren't showing up to school, and I couldn't even hold back my tears some days. The pain I was going through was horrible. I had to take slow and deep breaths to pass it. It helped that I could sit at my desk all day and look busy because, during this time, it was so hard to focus and concentrate on anything other than my daughter. If you are the mother of a child who has been through sexual abuse, I want you to know that I love you. You are an amazing mother and woman, and none of that was your fault. I'm sending you a hug right now. *Tu eres poderosa*: You are powerful. Please know that I'm here for you.

During this time in my life, while dealing with my daughter's traumatic situation, I realized that I was retriggered because of my own experience with sexual abuse as a young girl. I had not dealt with my own trauma, and I was under extreme pain and stress while trying to deal with what was happening to my daughter. I buried my past pain so deep within myself, and years later, I had to face and confront the pain that I had been carrying around. I had to start taking off my band-aids, but it didn't happen overnight. I needed to go to therapy to talk about this with someone. If you have experienced something similar and haven't dealt with it, I advise you to speak to a therapist. Therapists are so needed and necessary. Sometimes you just need to talk to someone you know won't go talk behind your back. I also want you to know that you are still worthy. What other people do or say to us doesn't change our worth or value.

You have been created beautifully, and even if others have hurt you, it doesn't change your worth. If you feel shame because of what happened to you, release it. The problem with shame is that it deceives you. Shame makes you think you're damaged goods, that you're ugly and worthless. Shame tells you if people knew what happened, they wouldn't love you. But shame is a liar, and for some reason, we start to feel comfortable with it and embrace it. Some of the shame we carry was never ours to begin with. If you are carrying shame around, it's time to evict it from your life. You didn't invite it in, so you don't have to let it keep hanging out with you.

This is why healing is necessary if you desire to become an empowered woman. If you want to be fearless, you have to have the tenacity to begin your healing journey. It doesn't happen overnight, and you might heal slower in one area than someone else, but all that matters is that you start somewhere. Life will throw unexpected curve balls at us. Everything is not rainbows and sunshine. We go through horrible and painful things in life, and there is no guarantee that we will always be happy. It's how you handle the curve balls that matters. It's how you deal with a traumatic situation and how you rise above it.

> You may encounter many defeats, but you must not be defeated. In fact, it may be necessary to encounter the defeats, so you can know who you are, what you can rise from, how you can still come out of it.
>
> — Maya Angelou[1]

Girl, encountering defeats will show you who you really are. You will see a whole side of yourself you didn't even know was there, and when you rise above it, it feels pretty amazing! So, think of your healing journey as something you are doing because you are ready to rise above. That's how you become fearless. When you rise above what looks like defeat, and instead, you come out of it.

Maybe you've come out of some things that were meant to defeat you, but instead, you rose above it, and now, looking back, you see how much stronger you are. If that's you, wow, I'm so proud of you. Maybe you have been through some things you can't seem to get past. Well then, we will do this together. Confronting the pain is not easy, but it's necessary. Healing looks different for everyone. For some, it means letting go of someone they loved, moving away to start a new chapter in their life or both.

Healing might also mean that you have to forgive those who hurt you. I know. No one wants to talk about forgiveness. Some people were raised to think that forgiveness makes you weak. The truth is forgiveness is the exact opposite of being weak. Forgiveness means you are strong because only a strong person can forgive when someone hurts them. Forgiveness gives you the power to let go and no longer hold on to the past. Forgiveness helps you release what was never yours to own, including the pain others inflicted on you. If you ask me my definition of forgiveness, I will say that forgiveness is a rare skill that only the strong possess. It takes time to acquire this powerful skill. It's not just for some people, anyone can attain this skill, but not everyone is willing to do that. Why am I calling it a skill? Because having a skill and mastering it takes time, learning to forgive also takes time.

Forgiving doesn't mean that you're saying what someone did to you is okay with you. It also doesn't mean you have to reconcile or be their best friend again. You must still have boundaries. It means that they are not your responsibility and that you will no longer give them power over you. That's why forgiveness must be part of the healing journey. Without it, you will carry around resentment, and trust me: it's not pretty. I know this because I hung out with resentment for way too long.

Amiga, I know how hard this part of the healing journey can be. Trust me, I know. I carried unforgiveness around for many years, and it never made me feel any better. Honestly, it caused me to feel more depressed than I already was. I replayed everything others did to me, and I could never let go of things that happened. Do you know why I had a hard time letting go and forgiving? It was because I put a band-aid on top of another band-aid. If something happened, I would shut that person out and call it forgiveness. Growing up in dysfunction and mental and emotional abuse, you will try to do whatever you can to survive and protect yourself. I became a master at shutting people out. Over time I have learned that if people have faded out of your life, it may be that they were only there for a season. I have learned that you should not tolerate toxic people, even family. You need boundaries in your life because you will be distracted and try to find validation in others without them. Forgiving is not easy and must be on your terms. Take the baby steps necessary to forgive those who have hurt you, and if you're not there yet, it's completely okay. Girl, please take your time.

I don't have a formula for forgiveness, and I am also not a forgiveness expert. But I have experienced my own journey of forgiveness, and I don't think that it's one-size-fits-all. I can tell you some of the things that worked for me on my way to forgiving others, but what I did may not work for you. I also have to mention that forgiving doesn't come naturally for me and was modeled by someone else. I come from a dysfunctional background, and forgiveness wasn't something I learned as a child. I learned about forgiveness as an adult because I watched my husband forgive things and never bring them up again. That's a sign that you have forgiven someone: you don't bring up what happened. I was the exact opposite. I would bring up something that happened ten or fifteen years ago. I have always admired this about my husband. He had a hard life growing up, and I've watched how kind, forgiving, and generous he's been. Being around someone like that will inspire your heart in ways you never imagined. Let me tell you, the guy isn't perfect, but this part of him I love. God knew that I needed someone like him. It's been refreshing and safe for me while I've gone through my healing journey. It's been a process, and I've had to take baby steps. Remember this, when you are ready to start forgiving, please take baby steps because this is not easy. Remember, please talk to a therapist because forgiving can be a triggering experience. I believe in you so much, *Amiga*.

I mentioned earlier that healing would mean you would have to be okay with being uncomfortable. Sometimes healing will require you to do things you are not comfortable with, and other times you might have to step into the unknown and let go of what you once knew. Think about when a woman's marriage ends due to infidelity, and she has to pick up the pieces. She must learn to adjust to a new way of life, and a marriage ending is never easy. There are many examples of *Mujeres* who have had to pick up the pieces of something horrible, and they had no choice but to keep going. Doing what's uncomfortable is what grows you and what makes you stronger. Doing what's uncomfortable will fill you with courage and bring you inner healing.

I have always felt it in my heart to help women. Back in 2016, I had this crazy idea to start vlogging, so I made a video about my journey with God, and after one whole day, I took it down. I wasn't in a good place emotionally. I was depressed and was on an emotional roller coaster. But the main reason I took it down was that I became bombarded with the same question over and over, *what are people going to think if they see my video?* You can't worry about what people think about what you do. Most people who have an opinion about what you do, are not following the dreams in their own hearts. If you're not pursuing that thing in your heart because of the fear of what others will say, it's time to start working on that. The fear of what others say is a huge stumbling block in your life.

In 2020, I felt this deep burden to begin sharing my stories with other women and encourage them. With the pandemic having just started, I began to think about the women who might be depressed and would have to deal with it in quarantine. One night I heard a woman preaching online about how our stories are meant to heal others. That's when I started believing that my stories could also help others. So, as I was on my healing journey, I began to make videos encouraging women.

Honestly, I don't like being on camera, and I don't like my voice. I think we can all be a little like that at times. We wonder if we really sound like that or look like that? I didn't start making those videos right away, but I felt led to encourage women somehow. You already know that my faith is a huge part of who I am. And if I can be honest with you, sometimes God will inspire you to do things out of your comfort zone. Sometimes you will have this thought, and you're like, where did that come from? It stays there, and you can't stop thinking about it, and as I like to say, it gets louder. What God inspired in my heart was to share my stories so that others could heal. I know it sounds crazy, but it's what I believed God put on my heart, and it quickly became the theme in my heart. But after making a few videos, I felt that it was not for me.

I don't know how the thought of starting a podcast came about, but I began to research everything that I could about podcasting. I watched hours of videos, read a ton of blogs, and started doing my homework. Then I borrowed my son's microphone and began to podcast. A few weeks after starting my podcast, I received a message on Instagram from a woman who had heard my first episode about depression. She said this episode helped her, and she was so thankful. After that message, I thought, *maybe I'm not crazy for doing this.* You see, I still had this fear of what people would think. But at that point, I started not to focus too much on that. I would receive random messages from women about different episodes. To me, it was God showing me that this was something I needed to keep pursuing. But let me tell you that starting a podcast is work. It's not like you just plug in the mic, and you're good. If you are a podcaster and reading this, I am not telling you something you don't already know. It's work, and expect to work hard when you embark on this journey. Why am I sharing this with you? Because as I began to share my stories and connect with other women, I began to heal more and more.

I learned that my voice was powerful, and I began to heal through using it. You might be like, but Micaela, that's not crazy? Girl, to me, it was. I never felt that my voice mattered, and honestly, I always said that I didn't want people knowing my business. Being a podcaster with an inspiring and empowering podcast will make you show up in your vulnerability t-shirt. My message was all about sharing my stories. Each time I shared a hard one, I would receive messages from women who had gone through something similar. I began to connect with a lot of women on social media I would not have met any other way.

Sometimes on the path to healing, you will start to do something you never knew you could do or that anyone needed for you to do. There were times I was very discouraged. I would share my episodes on social media, and it seemed that no one was interested in even clicking the like button. That can make you question yourself, but I've learned that you should never measure what you are doing based on how many likes you get. The world we live in today will make you think you're not doing anything significant if you don't have followers or likes. Don't let that fool you because trying new things always takes time, consistency, and a lot of fire inside of your soul to keep it moving. So, while I would get one or two likes or no likes at all on Facebook, I began to connect with friends and other podcasters on Instagram. It was pretty amazing! I began to feel free to use my voice and share my stories. That freedom began to heal me in a way that I am not sure would have happened any other way.

Maybe for you, it won't be that you start a podcast as you embark on your healing journey. Perhaps you will begin a Bible study if you happen to be led in that direction. Maybe you will start a book club to encourage women who need that. Maybe you have some *bomb* makeup skills and can teach women how to apply the best-winged eyeliner so that they can feel beautiful. Maybe your healing journey is about starting a baking business.

Whatever it is for you, do not limit yourself. Do what you feel is crazy and the thing that scares you. When you do it scared and keep doing it, you learn who you are and how resilient you are. If you ever felt that your voice didn't matter, I want you to know this; that is a lie. In the second chapter, I'll talk about lies that we believe and sometimes aren't even aware of. It's crucial to expose the lies you believe because they hold you back from living the life God intended for you to live. If you have ever believed that you had no voice and that it didn't matter if you used it, it's time to stop believing that. Repeat after me, "My voice is powerful, and it matters."

Things you will need as you embark on your healing journey:

- Courage to confront your pain and face your fears
- Willingness to be uncomfortable
- Strength to rip the band-aids off
- Openness to forgiveness
- Reminders that your voice is powerful

Trying new things always takes time, consistency, and a lot of fire inside of your soul to keep it moving.

Dear Fearless Mujer, You Were Created for More

Exposing the Lies

When you start to heal on the inside, you will quickly see that you don't just heal from one thing in your life. You begin to heal from so many things you didn't even know needed healing. The journey is not easy, but you see yourself like a completely new person once you start to heal. The best way I can describe this journey is that you experience a ton of pain in the beginning, and as some time begins to pass, slowly other parts of you begin to break off. The parts of you that break off were things you didn't need. Things that may have been holding you back. Letting go of someone you love so that you can heal can feel like ripping a part of yourself off. That's how bad it hurts, but as you allow yourself time to process, you begin to discover more about who you are. It wasn't easy for me to let go of my dad because I had such a deep attachment to him.

We went through hard times growing up. There were times we would count pennies just to buy a gallon of milk. I wrapped up shoe and soda can boxes with wrapping paper one Christmas. We didn't have money for presents, but at twelve years old, I wanted it to feel like Christmas anyway. Going through hard times like that will bond you with a person. I always felt like my dad got me, and I got him, and once he was no longer in my life, I didn't know who I was. I wanted to make him proud of me. I wanted him to be there for every milestone of my life. But I knew after this happened with my daughter, life wouldn't be that way. Some people grow up being taught that your family is your family no matter what, and we tolerate them just because they're our family. I used to think that too, but then I learned this mindset is way off. Yes, they are family, and yes, you love them. But, if a family member is toxic, then it is not okay to tolerate them.

Once my dad was no longer in my life, I began to discover new things about myself. You see, I was still going to my dad for his input, even as an adult. I wanted validation from him, and I wanted to please him. I wanted him to say how proud he was of me. Don't get me wrong, I still love my dad and what I am sharing with you is not to bash him. I share this with you because, as women, sometimes we try to find our identity in others. Sometimes we think, *well, this is who I am. This is how I was raised, and this is what I know.* When in actuality, it is the opposite. Sometimes we mimic what or who we saw when we were growing up, and we've embraced ideas, views, and mindsets given to us. We define ourselves based on someone else's idea or opinion of who we are. I am not sharing this with you based on my own experience. I am also sharing this with you based on what other women have told me. I have seen many women who have big dreams stop pursuing bigger dreams based on the fear that they are not good enough. That fear comes from what was spoken over them in the past. Sometimes the fear of not being good enough also comes from past mistakes.

I had to learn to do things without running to my dad. I realized that I had a hard time making decisions about things. I would sit on a decision to do something for days. It's almost like I was waiting for permission to do what I wanted to do. Now don't get me wrong, I have always been a little too independent because I have never wanted help from anyone. But we will always need help: Help from a mentor or coach to further our business, help from a friend to navigate hard things, help from someone when we need a word of encouragement. I had this belief that if I didn't ask for help, it made me look strong and tough. That's what I saw growing up, so I embraced that mindset as my own. Have you ever felt that way? *I got this. I'll just do this by myself.* Have you ever thought that a parent or someone would criticize you if you did something?

Amiga, I used to think that way. I realized that I constantly went to my dad for validation because he had high expectations for me. He was also someone who would criticize me constantly. I always wanted his input because I was trying to please him. Have you found yourself constantly trying to please a specific family member? You want that person to see, like look what I did? It's almost like when a little kid draws something on a paper and then wants his mom to turn around and say, "Wow, that's so pretty." We look for validation in others. We want them to say, *wow, that's so pretty.* We are looking for affirmation, and let me tell you, it is tough to learn to love yourself without affirmation.

When I speak of affirmation, I am not just talking about affirmations you say to yourself. I am also not talking about manifesting things in your life. The kind of affirmation I am talking about is the kind that brings transformation and renewal. Let me ask you a question, and please be honest. Have you ever felt like you weren't good enough because you were trying to accomplish something hard for you, but it looked easy for others? I used to struggle with comparison so much. I would look at other women and think, *wow, she has her life together and always seems happy.*

Even though I had faith in God, I still didn't know or have confidence in who I was. I had so many voices that spoke into my life. Other people's opinions always told me who and what I should do. When you try to fit into someone else's box, you will be miserable. You are trying to force yourself to be someone others want you to be. This is why affirming yourself and entering a season of renewal is necessary. If I asked you to tell me about yourself right now, you would probably answer with something like "I'm a mom" or "I'm the vice president of a company," or "I'm a teacher." Would you tell me who you are, or would you tell me what you do? When people ask me, "Who are you" my natural response is to say, "I'm Micaela, and I live in Texas." I have seen women have a hard time answering this question, and I wonder *why?* Why is it complicated for some *Mujeres* to answer that question? Could it be that we don't really know who we are? I learned that I had no idea who I was during my healing journey. I realized that I only saw value in myself if I took care of others or did something that seemed worthy. I also learned that my identity was wrapped up in my dad and how he raised me. I began to learn who I really was. It started with affirmations and learning to rewrite the lies I believed about myself.

One morning I was feeling so discouraged. I grabbed my *cafecito* and took it with me upstairs to my office. This was my *girl cave*, where I went to reflect. On this morning, I began to think about everything that had happened. As I prayed and thought about who I was, I began to write down my thoughts about myself. I wrote down twenty things, and when I was done, I began to read them back to myself. I realized that all of those twenty things I wrote down were lies. I believed lies my whole life, so whenever I tried to do something, I couldn't because there was a lie saying I wasn't good enough. As I read each lie one by one, I began to cry because I knew that none of that was true. Reading them aloud to myself made me cry because I was the one who wrote them down. It was my handwriting, and they were right there on my piece of paper. I knew that I needed to confront them. Sometimes we are not aware that we believe lies about who we are. Sometimes these lies have been so ingrained in our minds and hearts that we don't even know they are there, and we live our whole life captive to these lies.

We never get to be free to be who we really are because the lies are all we know. It's like walking in the same pair of shoes because they are the only ones you have. There comes a time when those particular shoes get old, worn out, and are no longer suitable for your feet. Do you continue to wear the same old shoes that are causing you pain and discomfort when you know there are better ones for you? Do you believe lies about yourself? Have you believed that you're not smart enough? Have you believed lies that you could never do something because you're a woman or that you could never be successful because you never finished school? There are so many lies as women we have come to believe. If you don't learn to start confronting and exposing these lies, you will never walk in truth. You will never be free to be who you were created to be. When you don't expose these lies, you will never see yourself for who you really are. The lies influence your view of yourself, affecting the decisions you make for yourself.

They won't just go away if you only try to get rid of them from a surface level. You have to dig deep.

When my husband and I bought our house, we had so many weeds in our front yard and backyard! If you have ever pulled out weeds, you know that they are tough to pull out, and if you don't pull it out at the root, it will just grow back. The reason home-owners hate weeds so much is because they kill your flowers and plants. Plus, they're annoying.

I remember we had this bush that seemed dead, so I told my husband to pull the whole thing out and get rid of it. He didn't want to and kept telling me that it was probably a rose bush. One morning we untangled the weed wrapped around it. We had to be careful because it was tight around the bush, but slowly we untangled it, removed it, and pulled it out. Pretty soon, some beautiful bright red roses began to grow. I was ready to get rid of it, and it turned out beautiful roses were waiting to grow. They couldn't grow because the weed was suffocating and killing the bush.

When I think about lies women believe, I picture this in my mind. The lies are wrapped so tight and close around a woman's dreams, and they are suffocating and killing those dreams. So how can you pursue the things in your heart if you don't believe you can do those things? There are dreams inside of you, ready to grow, but first, you have to begin to remove these lies. How many times have you gotten excited about doing something, but then a few days later, you start to think, *never mind, I can't do that*? This is because you have gotten used to living with these lies wrapped cozily around you.

Sometimes you can be like a beautiful plant, rose bush, or your favorite flower. You need to be watered, nurtured, and nourished. Maybe no one ever did that for you. Perhaps you didn't have a mother who nurtured you or affirmed you. Perhaps you come from dysfunction as I do, and you have no idea how to nurture yourself. You have to decide if you are willing to do the hard inner work. Are you willing to walk in a different way than what you are used to? Maybe it's time that you wear a different pair of shoes? Maybe it's time that you become okay with digging deeper into where the lies come from?

To become a fearless *Mujer*, you must face the things about yourself that might hurt. But if you are ready, this is the part where you'll get honest with the lies you've been believing. You must first remove them so that you can begin to water the things that have been suffocating within you, and some of those things are your dreams. What is your biggest dream? If you had no obstacles or challenges, what would be that one thing you would love to do? Just dream with me for a minute here. How would you feel if you were there next year? What would that be like for you? Your dreams are possible, but not without learning to see yourself from a whole new light.

Because the truth is, what you think about yourself matters. How you see yourself affects your decisions, and if you are a mother, it affects how you raise your kids. We project things onto our children without even realizing it. As women, sometimes we lead with our heart instead of our mind or what's true. When you learn to rewrite the lies you believe, you will learn to walk in truth and stop trying to lead from your heart. Your heart can deceive you, especially if it's carrying lies. It's time to lead from a place of the knowledge you have about yourself. What I mean is if your heart is telling you things like, "Someone said I couldn't have a business, and now I feel worthless and not good enough," you can challenge that. You can ask yourself, "Is this really true?" before you allow yourself to entertain that thought about yourself. You can challenge that feeling and put it alongside what you know to be true about who you are. This takes practice and time. Please give yourself grace.

Rewriting these lies is going to help you to renew your mind. What does it mean to renew your mind? When you renew your mind, you begin to think differently about yourself. So many women walk around seeing themselves through others' eyes, with the labels others have placed on them. Renewing your mind is necessary. It helps you get rid of old ways of thinking that can damage you mentally and emotionally. It will also help you so that you can begin to affirm yourself. If no one has ever affirmed you, you might feel a little weird, but this is where you can begin to nourish your mind and begin to walk in truth. By affirming yourself, you will begin to cover yourself in truths. It's like when you put your shirt on. You don't think about all the things you do to put it on. You just do it. This is what will happen when you cover yourself in truths. You will just begin to do it without thinking about how.

Let's start rewriting some of these lies. Don't just say them to yourself. Take a few minutes to write them down. It might be hard for you, and you may need to come back to this part, and that's okay. I'll be here! The women I have coached have told me how eye-opening this part of their coaching is because they can see the lies. Something powerful begins to happen when you are the one writing *your* lies. You are exposing the lies and, therefore, taking your power back. You are the one untangling the weed wrapped around you for too long. So, what is a common lie that you believe? My big lie was that I wasn't good enough. That I was a failure, and no matter what I tried, I would mess it up anyway, so what was the point of me doing it? Do you see how this could prevent me from pursuing the things in my heart? Do you see how I might not value who I am if I continue to walk in these lies? This is why you must rewrite these lies. The truth about these lies is that they prevent you from fully becoming the woman you were created to be. You see, no matter what others have said to you or about you, it has never changed the love God has for you. It never changed the purpose He put inside of you.

You have a bigger purpose, and it has been there since the day you were born. There is a Bible verse that says, "Before I formed you in the womb, I knew you before you were born, I set you apart; I appointed you as a prophet to the nations" (Jeremiah 1:5).

God was calling Jeremiah to be a prophet to the nations, meaning he would be one that would speak God's truth to others. Is it possible that God has already destined something special for each of us? I think it is highly possible. That is why some people are naturally good at things or feel burdened for something specific: they have a bigger purpose. We all have something to fulfill on this earth. You are not here by accident. You have been created on purpose and with a beautiful purpose. You have been designed so beautifully by your maker. It's time to rewrite these lies because they will flow into every area of your life if you don't. Lies turn into themes in our lives. A lie will become a theme that says, "I'm selfish for wanting to invest in myself." "I shouldn't waste my time on things for myself when I could do something else for my children." "I shouldn't start that business because I'm not smart enough, and it's too risky." "I'll just fail anyway, so why even try." These are only a few common themes that stem from lies we believe about who we really are, and guess what? Fear thrives on lies and lies feed the fear. It's crucial that you expose these lies and know that you have the power to remove these lies.

Are you ready to do this? Write down ten lies that you have believed about yourself. Once you write them down, it's time to rewrite them. Feel free to download the Fearless Mujer Empowerment Guide. It will help guide you as you begin to rewrite the lies. You can find the link in the Appendix.

LIES I BELIEVE:

_____

_____

_____

_____

_____

_____

_____

_____

_____

_____

I teach my coaching clients to use Bible verses to rewrite the lies. Here is an example: If you have believed that you are worthless, I want you to tell yourself, "I am worthy because _____ (fill in the blank.) I would use a bible verse that lifts you up like I am worthy because I am far more precious than jewels (Proverbs 31:10). or you can do it differently and say I am worthy because I'm God's masterpiece (Ephesians 2:10). My life has value because God says "I am fearfully and wonderfully made" (Psalm 139:14). If you are not comfortable using Bible verses, feel free to use inspirational quotes, or both if you like.

Let's take a quote by Maya Angelou as an example: ``You alone are enough, you have nothing to prove to anybody."[2] You can write I _____ (insert your name) am enough, and I have nothing to prove. You can also blend them if you like. If you want to blend them, you can write "I am more than enough because_____ "and then fill in the rest with a Bible verse that resonates with you and also add the inspirational quote. This is about you and how you choose to rewrite these lies. Before we continue, you're probably thinking, can this really rewrite the lies I have been believing? The answer is yes because these rewritten lies will become your affirmations and subconsciously interrupt how you view yourself. You can call it reprogramming, but I will call it renewing your mind.

As we continue with this chapter, you will see why it is so important to renew your mind, especially as you begin to pursue the dreams in your heart. These affirmations will become your truths. Bible verses are so powerful because they begin to align your view of yourself with what God says about who you are. We have been conditioned to accept what others have spoken over us.

We have embraced the negative opinions of others about who we are. These affirmations will begin to transform you and help you let go of the identity that others have placed on you.

Your thoughts and view of yourself influence how you choose to live your life. Proverbs 23:7 says, "For as he thinks in his heart so is he. Eat and drink, he says to you, 'But his heart is not with you.'" Now before you get confused, let me explain. What you see in this verse is a person who is saying one thing with their mouth, but their heart is not in agreement. Most of us tend to act on what we feel in our hearts. We agree with what we feel about ourselves and begin to think that this is just who we are. This will shape your thinking and influence your decisions for your life. What you feel about yourself becomes what you think about yourself, and it matters. It is shaping your view of yourself.

When you feel like you're not good enough and constantly say this to yourself, you believe you are not good enough. You're programming your brain to believe that. Your brain is so powerful that it believes whatever you tell it. It also repeats whatever you are saying. Be careful what you are feeding your brain. Your brain cannot tell if something is real or not. Think about this, have you ever had a triggering thought about something terrible that happened to you? That happens because your brain is remembering something traumatic, and you get triggered because it thinks it's happening at that moment. Your brain is powerful, and you need to be careful what you're feeding it. Think about a plant for a second; it needs water and sun to thrive in its environment because if it doesn't thrive, it will wither and eventually die. Your brain thrives when you nourish and nurture it. Remember the rose bush I mentioned earlier? You are like that rose bush that needs to thrive, and that's why it is so important that you begin to watch what you are saying about yourself. Your thoughts will influence how you choose to live your life. You have the power to tear yourself down with your words or build yourself up with them. You have the power to speak life into yourself. I know the concept of speaking life into yourself can seem weird if you've never lived by that. It can also feel weird if no one spoke life into you growing up. It's hard when no one has nurtured you in the past, but here is where you get to step in and do that for yourself. The more you speak life into yourself, the more you will believe in yourself. The more you will see yourself through new eyes.

When you speak life into yourself, you also teach others how to speak life into themselves, and your daughters, nieces, sisters, and cousins need that. Speaking life into yourself will help you renew your mind and fill you with love and gratitude for who you are.

When you learn to renew your mind, your self-perception will align with what God says about who you are. You will experience the freedom to be who you are when you no longer have the wrong mindset about yourself. But here is where it gets tricky: not everyone is aware of how they view themselves. Some women view themselves based on who someone else thinks they are. How you view yourself influences how you feel about yourself, and how you feel about yourself dictates your decisions. What you believe about yourself and think about yourself matters.

As women, we are juggling life and responsibilities. We wear so many different hats. We don't always take the time to get to know who we are as women or pay attention to our thoughts about ourselves. It is said that the average human has 12,000 to

60,000 thoughts per day. What a difference it would make if you had 60,000 good thoughts about yourself per day? That would be amazing, right? Think about this? When you feel hopeless, shut down, and not good enough, you're not able to make the impact you were put on this earth for. You have been created with a purpose, and when you hold onto negative mindsets, it blindsides you from stepping into what God has purposed for your life.

When you renew your mind, you will see yourself from a new lens and with a new perspective. You will no longer see yourself with an old lens of what has happened in the past or what people have said about you. Sometimes we might think, *well, this is just the way I am.* Maybe you've said that about yourself, circumstances, or a situation in your life. Maybe you've thought *this is just the way that my life is, and things will never change.* That kind of belief leaves you stuck. I used to think the same thing whenever I would experience challenging things in my life. Now I know this belief makes it more difficult to fully understand and process a difficult situation. When things are going wrong, you can change the angle you view these challenges from. Think about when you are watching TV, sitting on the couch, then you get up and sit on a different spot on the couch, and you notice something you didn't before. The belief that "this is just the way my life is" or "this is just the way I am," is a belief that limits you. This is what you call a limiting belief.

Let's dive into what they are and why people have them. Limiting beliefs are false beliefs about yourself and about your life. Limiting beliefs hold you back from living a life of wholeness and abundance because these false beliefs affect your decision-making and your ability to take risks. They offer you a view of what you can and can't do, and if you allow these beliefs to control you, it will be hard for you to accomplish your life goals. Limiting beliefs stop you from pursuing your goals and your dreams. They are a stumbling block in your life because they tell you who you are and what you can and can't do. It's like wearing glasses and trying to see, but you never have a clear vision because your view of your life is distorted because of these beliefs. Limiting beliefs stop you from reaching your full potential because they limit you. It's hard to believe in yourself when your beliefs are preventing you from doing so, and these beliefs always find a way to surface. So, where do these beliefs come from? How you were raised influenced what you believe about yourself and even how you see the world. Growing up, your parents or the people you looked up to more than likely projected their beliefs onto you. That includes their fears, doubts, and limitations. They molded your way of thinking.

Here's an example: maybe you've always wanted to start a business, but you're scared you will fail and think it's too risky. Why do you think that? Think back in your life, as far back as you can remember, who did you hear say things like: "I can't do that because I will fail or it won't work," or "I can't take a big risk like that." Did someone make you think you couldn't have something because of financial hardship? They constantly said there's no money, or we never have money? Because of that, you fear lacking money, and you constantly view things from a scarcity mentality. You worry that you won't have money if you invest in yourself, or maybe you feel selfish for wanting to go back to school or start a business. Maybe you think it's wrong to make your goals and dreams a priority. Have you ever asked yourself why you think that? These are only a few examples of limiting beliefs, and they can look different for everyone. Some women were constantly told they couldn't do or have something just because they were girls. That belief is carried into their adult lives. Were you ever told growing up that little girls don't do that or don't behave that way? Hearing that over and over as a young girl can condition you to believe that, and that belief becomes normal in time. You become accustomed to what is normal to those around you.

Have you ever compared yourself to a friend on social media or someone you know? I think we have all compared ourselves to someone else at some point in our life. The *comparison trap* is another way your self-image is shaped and molded by others. Falling into the trap of comparison leads you to believe lies about yourself, which can turn into beliefs that limit you.

Let's say that your parents or grandparents constantly compared you to a sibling or cousin, and no matter what you did, it seemed that you never measured up to that person. If you experienced that, comparing yourself to others might seem normal. You might believe the lie that you can't do something like someone else. Have you ever told yourself you couldn't do something because you weren't smart enough or educated enough? Maybe you've compared your life to someone else's. Maybe while scrolling through social media, you happen to notice another woman's profile or timeline, and you begin to compare yourself to her. Maybe you even say something like, "she has that husband because she's pretty," or "She has that job because she's smarter," or "she has that life because she's better than me." These thoughts you might think aren't a big deal actually are because they stem from something deeply rooted inside of you. And that something is a lie, the lie that says you're *just* a girl, or you're not smart or good enough.

You might even believe the lie that you can't have something because of where you grew up and where you come from. I call this the *that's not for me* lie. I used to believe this lie too. Years ago, when I used to drive in a neighborhood with nice houses, I would say, "that's not for me." I would say I could never have that because I was just a girl from the hood, and having a house wasn't meant for me. I also believed having a business wasn't for me. It took me years to stop believing this lie. This lie will cause you to self-sabotage in more areas of your life than you think. Other times the belief that *it's not for me*, or *that's not for me* will make you think you're being humble, but it's a false sense of humility. Because let's be honest, we all stare at beautiful houses because we desire to have a beautiful house, and there is nothing wrong with that.

When my husband and I bought our house, I saw this lie exposed before my very eyes. We sold our home and moved since then, but now I know that buying another home *is* for me, and it's not impossible. Do you have a *that's not for me* thing? Is it a house, a car, a business? If you have believed this, I want to challenge you to ask yourself where this belief came from? The truth is that *it is for you.* That house is for you. That car is for you and your dreams are also for you. It's time to believe this is possible for you. Start by writing down your dreams and asking yourself how to start taking steps to get there. Then take baby steps and give yourself grace while you do.

Don't compare yourself to anyone else. The comparison trap will distract you from becoming the *Mujer* you are meant to be. Lies like this are like weeds that need to be pulled out. If you don't pull these lies out at the root, you will live your life according to the lies you believe. The growth you want will not happen if a weed is holding onto you. Rewriting the lies you believe is a must if you desire to reach your full potential. Do you think a plant can grow if you never water it or give it sunlight? It can't grow because it's not receiving the nutrients it needs to flourish. You will also not grow and flourish if you walk in lies about who you are. If you have any dreams for a successful future, you need to know who you are. The truth is that these lies will limit every area of your life.

Do you ever get pumped and motivated about starting something, and then someone might say something about what you are doing, so then you stop? Because someone discouraged you? Have you listened to a motivational speaker or read a personal development book, and you became inspired to pursue your dreams? Were you intensely motivated for a few months or weeks but then the motivation suddenly disappeared? Have you ever asked yourself why that happened?

Look, *Amiga*, I will never tell you to stop reading books or listening to podcasts or motivational speakers, but these things can become a band-aid. Don't get me wrong. These are amazing tools. Still, without getting to the root of why your motivation only lasts for a little while, you will continue this spiral of temporary excitement and inspiration that only lasts a little while. When your perspective of who you are is mixed with lies and limiting beliefs, it will slow you down and eventually stop you from pursuing the dreams in your heart. Motivation and inspiration will not go deeper than what's on the surface when you believe lies about who you are. The lies you believe about yourself and the limiting beliefs you carry will steal your joy, kill your future, and destroy who you were created to be. I believe that there is a bigger reason why we have big dreams, and that's because we are meant to influence and inspire others through those dreams.

Another reason why you have limiting beliefs is the labels others have placed on you and the labels you have placed on yourself. For example, have you ever told yourself any of the following things?

- "No one even likes me."
- "I'm so stupid."
- "I'm always messing everything up."
- "I'm not that pretty."
- "I'm a failure."

Does that sound familiar to you? Have you stopped and wondered where these words came from? I'm not saying you are any of these things, but I want to show you how words like this stick to us.

I call these negative sayings *invisible labels*. I have to confess my obsession with Post-it notes before I continue. As a podcaster who creates unique content, I love having Post-it notes around. They're great to remind you of tasks, and I also love how sticky they are. This is what I think about when I think about labels: Post-it notes that are stuck to you with every awful lie you believe about yourself.

What if I told you that you have invisible labels stuck on you? We really do have them, and in fact, many women have them, and they don't even know it. These labels are lies and limiting beliefs. These labels tell you who you are and what you can and can't do. If your label says, "Not good enough," you will continue to walk around thinking that about yourself, and you won't reach your full potential.

My labels used to look something like this:

- "You always mess everything up."
- "You're a failure."
- "No one loves you."
- "No one wants to be with you."
- "Everyone else is smarter than you."
- "No one will ever marry you."

These labels can go deep into the innermost part of who we are. That's why it's crucial to identify these labels so that you can begin to remove them one by one. These labels will cause some women to hate themselves and never fully see themselves as the beautiful creation they truly are. These labels can destroy who you are meant to be. I'm not here to scare you, but I am here to expose these labels and lies so that you can be the one to take them off because you are the only one who can do this. And you must be willing to do this for yourself. Here is some truth for you: the things you speak over yourself and believe about yourself are often rooted in your heart and mind because someone spoke these things over you. You have learned to view yourself this way, believing these things about yourself. When you are carrying invisible labels, you will never experience the freedom of discovering who you really are.

Let me share something personal with you; my father would constantly criticize me when I was growing up. It felt like I never met the expectations he had for me. I made many mistakes, and one thing that was never evident in my upbringing was grace. I never knew what it meant to give myself grace when I made mistakes, so I always felt like a failure, and I believed that no matter what I did, I just wasn't good enough. I would beat myself up a lot whenever I made a mistake. I would tell myself I was stupid and I shouldn't even try to do whatever it was I was trying to do. I am not sharing this with you to feel bad for me. I am sharing it with you to know where I'm coming from. I had labels that I needed to remove off myself, but I was the only one who could do that. No one else could remove the labels for me. You must recognize what labels you have embraced that should not be a part of you. This is why you must rewrite the lies you believe so that they no longer stick to you because labels become lies we believe. These labels were put there without your permission, and now it's time to permit yourself to remove these labels.

We also carry labels we've embraced from our past mistakes. These labels become lies we believe about who we are. Have you ever made a mistake someone continued to remind you about? Have you ever tried to forget a mistake and others would continue to say, "Remember when you did that?" Here is a truth for you, your past mistakes do not define you, and no matter what others have spoken over you, you are not your mistakes. Unfortunately, there will be people who like to remind others of their mistakes. If you have ever been divorced, people will label you as the divorced woman. If your husband cheated on you, to others, you might always be the woman whose husband cheated on her. And if you did the cheating, you're the woman who is a cheater. People are so good at making up their own definition of someone else. But sometimes, we can tend to do that to ourselves.

There are times that we will place labels on ourselves based on our past mistakes. Let's say that your past relationships haven't worked out; you may label yourself as the woman who isn't good in relationships. If you've had a failed business, you might say, "I'm a failure when it comes to business." When you place labels on yourself based on your past mistakes, your perspective will be based on a lie because you've learned to define who you are by your failures. The labels you have placed on yourself are not true, and you no longer have to carry them around.

The truth is that your mistakes can become a message. Your mistakes can become what fuels your courage and tenacity to keep going. To have tenacity means that you grip something firmly. Can you grip your courage to keep going? You see, mistakes might make you stumble, but they will only break you if you let them. It's important to shift your view about what a mistake truly is. I'm not saying that mistakes aren't a big deal; what I'm saying is perspective makes a huge difference. Switch the angle you're seeing your mistakes from. Your mistake can be a message: teaching and bringing hope to others.

What past mistakes are you holding onto? It's time to change the angle you are viewing it from. There's a quote from Bruce Lee that I like, "Mistakes are always forgivable if one has the courage to admit them."[3] You see, that's the first step, acknowledge that you have made mistakes. Don't try to avoid that part of yourself.

We often want to hide from our mistakes or pretend they never happened. When you don't acknowledge your mistakes, you will not move forward in life. You'll stay stuck. One of the things my father taught me growing up was if I ever messed up, I needed to admit it. He taught me to own my mistakes, and I am glad he did. There is power in that. You might think owning your mistakes makes you look weak. It's powerful when you acknowledge them and try to understand why and how that mistake happened.

You will grow so much when you understand why you made that mistake. I believe there are two types of mistakes a person can make. For example, you forget to turn your signal on when you make a right turn. Maybe you forget to make that important call to a client. Maybe your boss tells you to send an email to someone, and you just forget. Those are the *oops* mistakes! But then there are the other mistakes. The ones you know you probably shouldn't make. You contemplate the mistakes for a few days, then give in. I will go to the extreme here. Say you are married, and you know you shouldn't talk to that other guy, but you do it anyway. Something like that is a *huge* mistake. I'm not here to make judgments. I want you to grasp the bigger picture of what I'm saying. Those types of mistakes are the ones we try to hide from. But they can become a message that brings hope to others. That kind of mistake can make you wiser, and you can use it to help someone else. Instead of hiding or running away from the crazy mistakes you have made, choose to forgive yourself and help others. Forgiveness can be hard to do. We discussed this in the first chapter.

Forgiving yourself for past mistakes can be difficult, but you will be free when you do. The truth is, your mistake was a teacher that taught you something important. Through my faith, I have learned God can use pain for a bigger purpose. Mistakes can be painful, so we try to run away or shove them deep within us. But doing that will only hold you captive. When you're held captive by your past mistakes, it's hard to focus and truly be who you were created to be. If you're like, "Micaela, that sounds great, but you have no idea what I've done." I get that, and you're right, I don't know. I am no different from you, and I have also made many mistakes I wish I could erase. Honestly, if there were a master's degree in the Art of Mistakes, I would have it on my wall. Not because I would be proud of them, but to remind myself of everything I have learned and how truly free I am. So, tell me, *what mistakes are you holding onto?*

> Mistakes might make you stumble, but they
> will only break you if you let them.

What mistakes are holding you captive? What mistakes are holding you back from being who you were created to be? What labels have you placed on yourself because of your past mistakes? It's time to start removing these labels. Here is an exercise that you can begin doing:

1. Identify your mistake and write down one to three things you learned from that mistake. This will help you reframe your view of that mistake. It will also help you let go of the mistake, so you don't have to continue carrying it around.

2. Make a list of all the things you can remember that others have said about you because of your mistakes. Is there a lie that you can identify because of that mistake? How can you begin to rewrite it?
3. Write down the truth about who you are. Doing this part might be a little triggering, so please take your time. You don't want to rush this part because it will take you some time to reflect on things. It's not easy to look back on things that have happened to us or that we have done, but it's necessary to do so you can heal and step into who you are meant to be.

I carried around many of my own labels I wasn't even aware of. Through prayer and my healing journey, I began to discover the labels I had embraced as my own. When my dad was no longer in my life, I felt like I could think for myself. I was in my thirties, and to say I wasn't thinking for myself sounds crazy, but it's true. As time passed, it seemed my father's voice was beginning to fade away. I was beginning to discover who I was, and I don't mean whoever I thought I was. I began to understand that even if my father wasn't in my life, I was still God's daughter.

Before I dive into this, let me tell you, my dad was always a part of my life. Up to this point, I could never relate to the girl who didn't have her dad in her life. Not having a father in your life can be so painful, especially when you wish you could share certain milestones in your life. I need to say this to you, if you have never had a dad in your life, please know that you are not *less than.* You are not unworthy or unlovable. You are so worthy, and God loves you. Some people have this perception that God is this mean God who punishes. But actually, "God is love" (1 John 4:16).

I'm not trying to have a Bible study with you, but honestly, it wasn't until I was able to see myself the way God did that I was free. For so long, I was trying to fit in the box of others. I was trying to be someone I thought my dad wanted me to be. Even as an adult woman who was married and had children, I was trying to be someone who I thought somebody else wanted me to be. This caused me to walk around with a false identity. When you walk around with a false identity, you will try to live in a way that pleases others, even if it means not being true to who you are. What if God has more for you? What if you're not crazy for believing there is more for your life? What if your big dreams aren't so crazy? What if your dreams were put in your heart by God?

When I speak about your big dreams and being true to yourself, I'm not talking about being enlightened or anything like that. I'm talking about aligning your view of yourself with who God says you are. Once I was able to see myself the way God saw me, everything changed. You see, sometimes we do things based on what we believe that others will think or say about us. We don't want to be judged or talked about. Sometimes we make choices based on the validation others will give us, and sadly, we dim our light to make others comfortable. We are careful not to shine too bright. We also live according to what we have been conditioned to think. What if you knew you had no limits to what you could accomplish in this life? What if the opinions of others didn't bother you anymore? What if you believed you could do the very thing that has been on your heart? What if, instead of worrying about what others thought of you, you began pursuing your goals and dreams because you knew people were cheering for you? You probably wouldn't doubt yourself anymore; you would just believe you could do it. Here is the truth about pursuing your dreams, everyone isn't going to support you. Sometimes it will have nothing to do with you but more to do with who that person is. And sometimes, you will have to be your biggest cheerleader, coach, and friend.

Not having my dad in my life was a painful moment, and it has been the most painful to this point in my life. It left me with unhealed wounds, unanswered questions, anger, grief, and confusion. It also caused me to confront the lies and labels I was embracing. I discovered why I had embraced certain labels and why I believed certain lies about myself. People say the past is in the past. If that's true, why are so many women afraid to be who they really are? I've heard people say, "just get over it," and if it is easy, why are women still wounded from their past? Why are they walking around too afraid to pursue the dreams in their heart?

I know this is a deep question, but it's worth trying to understand because so many women want more for their lives because they know their lives are meant for more. Before you can step into *more* for your life, you must ask yourself an important question: "Who am I?"

Maybe you have experienced something traumatic as an adult, a life-changing event, and you've had to ask yourself this question at some point. Asking yourself, "Who am I?" is not easy to answer because it forces you to look deeper. It forces you to look deep within yourself and beyond your circumstances. The trauma of what happened with my daughter forced me to ask this question, and it wasn't easy to answer because I didn't know who I was. I was a mother, wife, daughter, sister, but besides my roles and titles, I wasn't sure of who I was. If you have a hard time answering this question, I want you to know I understand, and you are not alone. Many women have a hard time answering this question. We are conditioned to believe our worth and value come from serving others. Serving others is meaningful, but that's not what makes anyone more worthy or valuable. Some *Mujeres* got so busy learning to juggle life and responsibilities they never had the chance to look deeper and ask, "Who am I?" Life-changing events can be a blessing in disguise because they will force you to look deep within yourself.

When this devastating situation happened with my daughter, I learned some things about myself. First, I learned that I was more than who I thought I was. I wasn't the mistake lingering over me, and I wasn't what others had said that I was. I learned that my voice and story were powerful and that other women needed to hear my stories. Second, I learned that I would always be my father's daughter because biologically, I was his. But, looking beyond what I could see on the surface, I realized that God had chosen my father and mother so I could be here because there was a much bigger purpose for my life. I realized there was a purpose for my life and the pain. So even though I had parents who created me, I understood the God who had a purpose for me created the two people who made me. Third, I learned I was who God said I was, not what others said I was, and I learned I didn't have to stay stuck in the pain of what happened to me.

Mujer, I am not a therapist, but I have experienced much pain. When you're dealing with painful circumstances, you have a choice to make. You can stay stuck in your pain or move beyond it to heal and to help others heal. You have no idea what greatness your pain will be used for. Right now, it may not feel that way for you, but if you allow yourself to heal and allow your pain to have its own purpose, you will be amazed at how your story helps others. Your voice and story are powerful. You are powerful. God can take your mess and create a beautiful message out of it. Isaiah 61:3 says that He will give a crown of beauty for ashes. God will bring joy out of the sorrow in your life. Wherever you are right now, trust that there is more for you.

He will give you a crown of beauty for ashes.

Believe that no matter how messy things look in your life, there is so much more. It's like when you bake a cake. You get a beautiful and delicious cake from the mess and raw ingredients after being put through heat. Sometimes our process is messy, and we have to experience what feels like a hot mess, but without that hot mess, you won't experience the beauty of the cake. So, *Amiga*, are you ready to ask yourself, "Who am I?" Are you ready to experience the power of knowing who you really are and who God says you are? If you are, please know I'm here for you as you begin to explore this. If you are not ready, I will be here when you are. I want you to know you don't have to do this alone. I'm here for you as a friend, mentor, and coach. I have your back, and I'm cheering for you.

Before I continue, I want you to know you don't have to rush through your healing journey. You can take as long as you need to. And know it's okay to feel like you're not okay. This is not a race to see who can heal the quickest: this is a journey where you get to grow, evolve, and see yourself as the woman you were created to be. The most important thing I learned from my journey is that I am still a daughter because I am God's daughter. If you have never heard the concept of being God's daughter, that is something for you to explore. You may not believe in the God stuff, and that's okay. I am not here to push my beliefs on you.

Maybe you were hurt by people who were part of religion, or maybe you experienced *church hurt*. I want to be sensitive about that if that's you. I am not trying to convince you of something you don't believe, but if you are reading this, I believe you want the raw, honest truth. *This is my truth.* I began to see myself as God's daughter. My identity was so wrapped up in my father, and I believed so many lies about myself I couldn't see myself as who I was created to be. I wasn't created to embrace lies about myself, walk in half-truths, or hide in my pain. I was created to be a leader, mentor, empower others, and lift up my sisters.

I found my *real identity* as God's daughter, which gave me a new perspective I didn't have before. But, of course, that would never have happened without the mess I went through. Let me just say this to you, God's daughters come in all shapes, sizes, and colors. But each one reflects His light. This is who I see when I see you and all the other women who are part of The Fearless Mujer Sisterhood. I see someone God created. A daughter He has filled with purpose. That is why I don't ever allow myself to judge because I know each one of us has gifts, talents, and dreams waiting to be birthed.

So, who are you, *Amiga*? Who do you want to be? The beauty of this life is you don't have to stay stuck or keep reliving the past. Regardless of what has happened or what others have said about you, your past does not define you. The hurtful words of others do not define you. There is so much more for you, but you must be willing to look beyond your past. Your pain and mistakes do not define you. Do you believe there is more for you? The truth is you don't need permission to start living the life you were created for.

God's daughters come in all shapes, sizes, and colors.

No Necesitas Permiso

Have you ever been frustrated because you felt like there was more for your life, but you didn't know what that *more* was? I used to feel that way too. I felt so frustrated because I wanted to do more with my life, but I always felt like I wasn't good enough. It made me resentful when I saw other people doing amazing things because I wanted that. I had a deeper desire to do amazing things. But I didn't know how to go after the things in my heart.

If I'm being honest, I didn't know what I was going after, so I did what most people do and tried different things. I would get excited to try new things, but the lie that I would fail would replay in my head, and fear would take over me. I also didn't trust myself, and it was as if I was waiting for someone to tell me that it was okay to go ahead and go after that thing. I was waiting for validation.

I wanted those closest to me to notice me and tell me that I was worthy of more. I didn't realize it then, but I was waiting for permission from others to pursue the things in my heart. I always worried about what others would think about me if I decided to go after what was in my heart. I would be filled with anxiety thinking about what they would say. I was like the little girl pulling petals off a flower saying, "He loves me, he loves me not," except that for me, it was, "Should I do this or should I not?"

Can you relate? Have you ever worried about what others would think if you pursued a dream or a goal? Have you felt frustrated because others tried to dictate how you should live your life? Was it hard for you to decide something without another person's approval? It's especially hard when you have grown up with criticism. You begin to question, overthink, and doubt yourself. Self-doubt is a killer! It makes sense why it would be hard to make a decision when self-doubt is hanging out with you. Self-doubt is a complete lie that makes you feel like you're not good enough and manifests in other areas of your life. When you're struggling with self-doubt, you might not take a chance on trying something new. If you do try something new, you might walk away from it because you don't feel confident or sure of yourself.

When self-doubt is hanging out with you, it's easy to seek validation from others because you want to be seen and heard. It's hard when you feel like no one truly sees you for who you are. This is why learning to affirm yourself is so important. It will change the way you see yourself. In the next chapter, I will be diving into knowing who you are at your core. If you know that your life was meant to shine, it's important to discover who you are at your core. Knowing this will help you walk in authenticity.

I've learned that women want and need a safe place to go when struggling. Each *Mujer* wants to know that she isn't alone on this journey of self-discovery, evolving and growing. If you have ever felt alone, I want you to know that you're not. This book is your safe space. It's where you can be yourself and reflect on who you want to be. Can I be honest with you? I was a runaway growing up. All I ever wanted to do was run and hide my whole life because I never felt safe. Maybe you are thinking,

Why would you run away? Or maybe, *Wow, I can relate.* The truth is that when you grow up in dysfunction, sometimes it will make you feel like running and hiding. Not trusting those around you will also make you feel like running and hiding. I'm just sharing my own experience because I carried this runaway girl with me for so long. When things got hard or I felt inadequate about something, I would quit, run away, and not look back. If you have been through something similar, I want you to know there is no judgment here. As I said, you are safe here. Listening to the voice of others and their criticism will also make you feel like running and hiding. Maybe you can't relate, but bear with me, please, because there are a lot of *Mujeres* who have felt like running and hiding whenever things got hard for them. Running away from the hard things is never a good idea! Pursuing your dreams is not easy. It's understandable to feel like running away when things get hard or when the naysayers say that you can't do what it is you want to do. You will have to promise yourself that you will stay committed to following your dreams no matter how hard it gets or what others may say. It's so easy to replay the words of others and then give in to what they say.

If you have hopes and dreams to inspire and influence others, you must accept pursuing your goals and dreams will not be easy. Nothing worth having or doing is ever easy. That's why most people won't dare step out of the box they are in. They do what is acceptable to others, what is expected, and what is most comfortable. It's comfortable when everyone else agrees with you. Let me share an example with you. Let's say that you are the first one in your family who wants to start a business. You decide to go after this idea, and you're excited. Your family tells you it's not a good idea. They give you many reasons why it's not a good idea. They mean well and probably have valid reasons. So, you decide not to do it because of what others are saying. How do you feel once you decide not to pursue starting your own business? If you are sad or discouraged, it's because not doing something based on what others say is like trying to fit inside someone else's box. When we try to fit inside the box others try to put us in, we become frustrated. Ask yourself, are you trying to force yourself inside a box someone laid out for you? Over time you may have made decisions based on what others wanted for you. After I realized I had been trying to fit into the box someone else wanted me to be in, I was constantly in conflict with myself.

The main reason was I didn't feel I could be myself or openly talk about my dreams without knowing if I would be criticized. The box I am speaking about symbolizes every time someone tried to mold you into who they thought you should be. It's extremely conflicting when you follow someone else's definition of how your life should be. It's also frustrating when others try to minimize your dreams and waiting for others to see your vision for your life can be exhausting.

Remember, I am not a therapist or a psychologist. I'm a coach, mentor, mother, wife, entrepreneur, writer, and a *mujer* who has overcome painful things. I am sharing with you what I've learned from my own experience and things other women have shared with me. The box others tried to put me in was uncomfortable. It caused me to be a people pleaser, not have boundaries, and beat myself up when I felt that I didn't meet other peoples' expectations of me. It also caused me to make decisions based on the fear of what others would say. I grew frustrated because I wanted it to seem like I had it all together. I was self-sufficient, which came from years of trauma and dysfunction, and honestly, I am still working on not being self-sufficient. Becoming aware that you have been making decisions based on fear of what others will think or say if you decide to do what's been in your heart is a difficult moment. You might feel like you've been duped or even like you've let yourself down. If you have been through this, I want you to know you are courageous. It takes guts to stand up for yourself and be true to who you are.

God designed you in a unique way and for a specific reason. You're not meant to play small, live in fear, or be a people pleaser. God created you for a specific purpose, and it is more than what other people may have told you. Sometimes it's hard to accept and believe that you were created for more, especially if you have grown up in dysfunction and abuse. Growing up in an environment like that, conditions you to believe lies about who you are. Therefore, affirming yourself and renewing your mind is necessary.

Think about it this way, *if you have a greater purpose beyond what others can see, why would you want to live your life based on what others say?* Living your life and making decisions to please others is like being captive. You become captive to the opinion of others and will never be free to be who you were created to be. You are meant to live free from people-pleasing, free from the worry of what other people think, free from judgment. The truth is people are not perfect, and they will let us down. Yes, we all need support and advice at times, but the voice of others should not be our lifeline. You have to give yourself permission to be the *Mujer* God created you to be.

I mentioned Jeremiah 1:5 in the last chapter, "Before I formed you in the womb, I knew you before you were born, I set you apart; I appointed you as a prophet to the nations." That verse always speaks to my heart. God had already planned something for Jeremiah before he was ever born. He purposed Jeremiah to be His messenger, and that's powerful. His purpose was to be a prophet to the nations. Prophets were such unique individuals because they would speak messages to a particular group of people according to divine inspiration from God. But the part of this verse I love is the beginning where it says, "before I formed you in the womb, I knew you." God already had a plan for Jeremiah before he was born, and I believe God has a plan for us too. It's a beautiful message I hold on to because it reminds me that despite my pain, mistakes, or what others have said about me, my purpose doesn't change. You see, we don't need anyone's permission to fulfill our purpose.

Amiga, you have a purpose, and it doesn't matter what has happened in your life. It doesn't matter what mistakes you have made or what anyone has said about you. There is a reason why you are here right now, and I also believe you are reading this book for a reason. You don't need anyone's permission to pursue your dreams. Even if you have struggled with people-pleasing and seeking validation from others, you don't have to continue living this way. It's time to make yourself a priority and put yourself first!

For so many years, I felt that if I wasn't constantly serving everyone else, I wasn't good enough. If I wasn't a self-sufficient woman, that meant I was a failure. If I had not cleaned my home, made dinner, and served my husband, I had failed. I believed this lie for so many years, and I wish someone had told me I didn't have to live my life that way. I would have enjoyed my children more if I wasn't stressed out about things that I didn't need to stress out about. But this was ingrained inside me because I was raised with deep cultural beliefs. When I speak of cultural beliefs, I'm speaking about my father raising me with certain customs, ideas, and behaviors acceptable to him because of our culture. I wouldn't say that we followed every Mexican or Latino tradition. But, as the daughter of an immigrant, specific things were expected of me. I would imagine my father wanted to keep his culture and tradition alive. We weren't just Mexicans by ethnicity, but we were proud of our roots in our hearts. I am proud of my roots and proud to be a Chicana.

My father came to the United States in search of a better life, and I saw him work hard. I learned many things from him, but it wasn't easy. I was expected to do things at an early age I believe were necessary. However, I also believe there were better ways of going about it. I'll share an example with you. My father taught me how to cook when I was very young and told me I needed to learn so that when I grew up and was married, my husband wouldn't hit me. *Read that again.* In what world is that okay? In what world is it okay to instill in a little girl that she has to perform and meet certain expectations or endure harsh punishment? You are programming a child to think abuse is okay. Sadly, many young girls go through this, not just in other countries. It's happening in the United States. There were expectations set for me, and I was raised with an iron fist. Before you get the wrong idea, I am not here to talk bad about my dad, *this is my truth,* and this is part of *my* story.

I learned at an early age that certain things were expected of me, and I had failed if I didn't measure up. When I didn't meet the high expectations I had set for myself, I would treat myself horribly. I had a mean negative self-talk game going on. I would tell myself I was "garbage, a loser, a failure, a stupid girl," and more. I would beat myself up for days and fall into the vicious cycle of comparison. I lived captive to my negative thoughts and lies. I was in bondage with mistreating myself and neglected to see myself as the precious young woman I was. The sad reality about living this way is people will treat you the way you treat yourself. I wish someone would have told me I was worth so much more than being treated this way. When you are treated this way as a little girl, you believe this is what you deserve. It becomes what you know, so you accept this from those around you, and sometimes you might even expect it.

I'm not a parenting expert, but the *iron fist* parenting style doesn't work. It intimidates, scares, and fills the heart of a child with discouragement, especially for a little girl who longs to feel special, loved, seen, and heard. When you are being raised to perform, meet expectations, or endure harsh punishment, you do not feel seen, loved, and heard. You feel like something is wrong with you, and that's where the lie is planted. If you don't meet this expectation, then you're not worthy of love. If you don't follow my ways, you will endure harsh punishment. When this is the message you receive as a child, you become captive to your confusion and distorted view of who you are. Do you know what else some cultural beliefs do? They keep you silent. Were you ever told that little girls don't act like that? Little girls don't talk like that? Just sit there, be quiet, and look pretty, or *calladita te ves más bonita?*

When my daughter told my husband and I what was happening to her, I didn't realize it then, but I was retriggered. I was a victim of sexual abuse, too, but I never dealt with it. I never went to counseling because, in my family, we didn't tell people our business, and there was this belief that counseling was just for "crazy people."

At fifteen, I had been sexually abused by a family member, and when my father confronted this person, he denied it. That was painful, but what was most painful was this person was still allowed to live with us in our home. Every day, I had to see his face and see the same disgusting hands that touched me. My dad still hung out with him. Talk about not being seen or heard. I saw this man at family parties, and it wasn't just a reminder of what he did to me but also a reminder that I had not been protected. I've heard from so many women that when they experienced sexual abuse, they too were told to keep quiet. Some were not believed, and others were blamed. This book is not about sexual abuse, but this is what fueled me to begin opening my mouth. As long as we stay quiet about things like this, we will never be free. As long as we allow ourselves to stay silent, our daughters will never be free. The generational beliefs taught to us as young girls that we have to show face and silence our voices are trash. Your voice can change the next generation.

> As long as we allow ourselves to stay silent, our
> daughters will never be free.

For so long, I functioned like that little girl, the one who was waiting to be seen. I often felt I had no voice, and I always felt like I was silently screaming inside. When you are raised to meet the expectations of others, you will never be the person God intended you to be. We cannot live our lives based on how others tell us we should. When we have been conditioned to meet the expectations of others, sometimes it's hard to outgrow that.

We become women who still carry around the little girl version of who we were, hoping to be seen and heard. We become adult women who conform to how the little girl we used to be would respond or react. This was something I had been experiencing, and the reason for this goes deeper. It can be because of trauma, dysfunction, abuse, and more. I won't go too deep into that because I am not an expert on trauma. But I am an expert on my own story, and I have experienced trauma and abuse. I am sharing this with you because if you have experienced anything similar, I want you to know you are not alone. There's always a deeper reason why we function or react the way we do. If you have ever felt like something is wrong with you, please know that is a lie. I don't know your life or what you've gone through, but I do know the belief that something is wrong with you is a complete lie. If you question if something is wrong with you and are constantly trying to meet the expectation of others, know you can start to live differently. *Amiga, tú no necesitas permiso*, you don't need permission to live your life the way you envision it. You don't need permission to pursue your goals, dreams, and more for your life.

The truth is, you were created for more. What does more look like for you? What are some of the things you would like to pursue? If nothing was holding you back, where would you be in the next six months to one year? How would your life be different? How does it make you feel to think your life can be different? Whatever your answer is, I want you to know you can do all those things. You can be exactly who you envision yourself to be! If you don't have an answer now, it's okay. Sometimes it takes time to get clarity regarding our goals and dreams. The most important thing is acknowledging you desire more for your life. This is how you can begin taking steps to get there. So, what do you want, *Amiga*? It's time to start asking the deep questions that will challenge you to go deeper and explore this. The beauty of this life, *of your life*, is that you get to choose what direction your life goes. You get to choose what's next for you. Before you begin this exploration journey, you must do one key thing. *Are you up for the challenge?*

If you said yes, I'm so proud of you! If you're not ready, stick with me a bit longer. Here is the challenge, will you love yourself enough to put yourself first? Discovering what's next for your life and going deeper will require you to love yourself and put yourself first. You have to make space for yourself because this has nothing to do with anyone else. This is about you and what you desire for your life. If you're thinking, "Micaela girl, that sounds so selfish." Yes, it is a little selfish. You have to be a little selfish for a better cause. Your decisions, goals, and dreams will influence the next generation of women. You may be the one called to pave the way for your daughters, nieces, cousins, sisters, etc. You being selfish for a more significant cause is okay.

By putting yourself first, you love yourself, and when you genuinely love yourself, you can love others better. I'm not saying you should neglect your family and stop prioritizing them. If you are a mother or responsible for others, you must stick to your commitments. However, it's time to make space for yourself. It's time to create boundaries so that you can do this. Creating boundaries will help you not feel guilty or bad for putting yourself first. It's crucial that you also make yourself a priority. You are important, worthy, and valuable. Your goals and dreams are also important, worthy, and valuable.

I want you to say to yourself, "I am important, worthy, and valuable." Then, write it down and put it where you can see it, so you never forget that.

> You have to give yourself permission to be the
> Mujer God created you to be.

Dear Fearless Mujer, You Were Created for More

There Is More to Who You Are

If I were to ask you who you are, would you be able to answer me? Could you tell me who you are without telling me what your titles are? Could you tell me who you are without telling me what you do? Would you believe me if I told you that this is hard for many *mujeres* to answer? So many *mujeres* attach their identity to what they're doing or who they're serving. As women, we wear so many different hats. We take care of others and have a lot of responsibilities. If you were the oldest daughter, you probably had to take care of your younger siblings and maybe even your parents. You learned to care for others before yourself and put the needs of others before your own needs. And that is a noble and selfless thing to do. But when you have embraced this role, it becomes what you know. Like I said, caring for others and serving them is a noble thing. It's beautiful when you care so much about others that you willingly and selflessly give of yourself. But it's dangerous when a woman measures her worth and value only by what she does or who she is taking care of.

Being in that place can quickly cause you to lose yourself. I have coached women who find it difficult to answer the question "Who am I?" It's not a bad thing, and I don't judge them for it.

But, I encourage them to dig deeper into this question. If it's hard for you to answer that question, then it's time to discover the answer. Now is the best time to begin reigniting the woman you are. If you have ever lost yourself and wondered, "Who am I now?" then it's time to begin the journey of reigniting the woman you are.

The process of reigniting the woman you are can also happen when you enter a season of change or a transition in your life. Because we are constantly evolving as women, we must reignite who we are. Once you learn to dig deep and ask yourself questions like "Who am I?" and "What do I want from my life?" you can begin to reignite the *mujer* you are.

Have you ever felt like you lost yourself, and you're not sure why or how that happened? One day you realize you're not the person you were before. Maybe you are dissatisfied with the way your life is? Maybe you've even lost your joy, and you don't know who you are anymore? I am going to go a little deeper, and I am sorry if I trigger you. That's not my intention. I love you, and I have to go here because I love you. Maybe you've even stopped caring about how you look, and you're wondering how you got to this place? For example, when you're a mom with little kids, it's easy to get caught up in taking care of them that you lose yourself. If you're married or have a significant other, maybe you've gotten too caught up in the relationship. Maybe your spouse has big dreams, and you've wrapped yourself up in their dreams, and you've lost yourself. This is not the case for every woman, but please don't feel bad if this is you. This is common for so many women.

We get so caught up in what is going on around us we can find ourselves wondering, *What happened to me?* It's tough when you come to that place in your life, but it can also be a good thing. You have a chance to begin the journey of rediscovering who you are. The truth is that there is more to you than what you do and who you serve. You are more than a mom, wife, girlfriend, employee, or business owner. You are more than what your titles say you are, and your titles are not your identity.

In this fast-paced society where we are constantly on the go, it's so easy to forget the person we are. In a world where we are told what is beautiful, strong, and worthy, we can quickly lose the woman we are. How many women who have been abused walk around with deep, unhealed wounds? We walk around as wounded women who may never have the chance to freely be who God intended us to be. Trauma and abuse have a way of confusing us into believing we are someone we're not, and we may never get a chance to truly experience the beauty of who we are. We become who we think others want us to be, someone acceptable and pleasing to them. Many women are carrying their wounded little girl around without realizing it. We carry her around and constantly see everything from her point of view. When you heal, you will find the freedom to be who you are meant to be, and you also discover there is more to who you are than what you do. When we continue to live without the inner healing needed, we have a distorted view of our identity. That's a huge reason we confuse our identity with our titles.

There is so much more to who you are at your core. There is a central, most important part of who you are. Let's take an apple, for example. When you go deeper into the apple on the inside, you find its core, and in the core are the apple's seeds. The seeds are where the minerals are and where the apple comes from. Once you plant those seeds, they can begin to grow. There is so much more to that apple. At your core self is your personality, beliefs, your inner wisdom. When you understand who you are at your core, you will step into a new boldness you may never have thought you had.

Understanding who you are at your core is not about changing who you are. It's more about revamping the woman you are. It's about getting honest with yourself to make decisions based on who you are and what you want, not what others think you should do. Not knowing who you are at your core is frustrating because you will continue to listen to the voice of others instead of your own. Other people's opinions begin to dictate your choices for your life. I am not saying you shouldn't seek advice or allow others to guide you. That is a wise thing to do. But, if you are making decisions for your life based on what others tell you they think you should do, that can be a dangerous place to be in, mainly because you will keep waiting for others to validate you, your goals, and your dreams.

When you do not truly understand who you are deep down inside, you will fail to set healthy boundaries that protect you from people-pleasing and becoming a *yes woman*. A *yes woman* has a tough time saying no to others, but saying no when necessary gives you the freedom to say yes to more important things. It's hard to say no when you haven't set healthy boundaries. Setting healthy boundaries is challenging when you don't know who you are at your core. If you're new to boundaries, I recommend exploring what that looks like for you. Boundaries will protect you from putting too much on your plate. When it comes to your life goals, boundaries will be essential. When you create healthy boundaries, you are also creating space for yourself. Often this is why women feel guilty about making time for themselves. It's because they have not yet identified what boundaries they need in their life. A great way to begin creating healthy boundaries is to identify your non-negotiables.

Having clear non-negotiables is an essential tool for setting healthy boundaries. It will also spare you from burnout and over-whelm. Your non-negotiables will help you clarify what you will and will not do. Non-negotiables are beliefs and values you will not go against. An example of a non-negotiable could be not al-lowing toxic people to influence your life decisions. This becomes something you choose not to go against. When you give toxic people access to your life decisions, you might become mentally and emotionally drained. Having a clear non-negotiable about your goals will help you accomplish them much quicker. For ex-ample, setting a non-negotiable for yourself when it comes to not allowing anyone to distract you from accomplishing your goals can be highly beneficial to your life. Define your non-negotiables and commit to them. Setting boundaries won't be as tricky once you define those for yourself.

Understanding who you are at your core is much more than just knowing who you are. Knowing who you are at your core will help you step into your authority so that you can confident-ly pursue the dreams in your heart. You will pursue your goals based on what you want and not what others want for you. You can begin to discover who you are at your core by identifying your strengths and weaknesses. Get clear on what your values and non-negotiables are. These are just a few examples that can help you begin understanding your core self so that you can step into your authority. In chapter six, I'll share more about your authority.

So, let me ask you something? Who do you want to be? If it was up to you, who would you be right now? Maybe you've been trying to be who others have told you that you should be? Maybe you're not pursuing the bigger dreams in your heart out of fear of what others might say if you begin pursuing what's on your heart? Maybe you believe the lie that tells you that you could never do that or have that because of your past mistakes? And maybe someone constantly brings up your past mistakes? Let's take that away for a minute. Dream with me. Use your imagination.

If you were not worried about what others might say, or if you couldn't remember your past mistakes, who would you be right now? What dreams would you pursue? What goals would become a priority for you? Sometimes it's hard to answer that question because of the pain, mistakes, and trauma we've experienced. Have you ever heard anyone say, "It's too late for me? I'm old now." or "I have kids now I can't do that anymore." Those are limiting beliefs and are also lies that people believe. I don't believe that where a person is going in life is ever set in stone because we are constantly evolving and growing. Who you are at twenty-five is not the same as at thirty-five. Your goals will evolve, too, if you allow them to evolve with you. If you hold on to the false belief, "well, this who I am" or "It's too late for me now," then you will never get to experience what you're capable of, and you will feel stuck.

Sometimes we put limits on ourselves. You would be surprised to discover what you could accomplish if you consciously choose to push yourself and stretch your limits. Having a clear vision of who you desire to be will help you identify what you need to do to get there. Having a clear vision about who you desire to be will also prevent you from comparing yourself to other women.

In this social media culture we live in, comparing ourselves to others comes easy. Everything is literally at the touch of our fingertips. There are many reasons why some women don't have a clear vision of who they want to be. Sometimes our circumstances become a stumbling block to where we are trying to go. Life gets complicated, and problems begin to weigh us down. Some women are constantly afraid of what others will think if they pursue an unconventional goal or dream. Other women give in to the fear that controls them. Thoughts like *What if I fail?* or *What if I'm not good enough to do this?* can stop you from reaching your full potential. Women who go through this become captive to negative thoughts and circumstances. If this is your situation right now, please know I am not judging you.

I have been there, and I speak from experience. I have compared myself, doubted myself, given into the fear of what others would think of me, listened to the voice of others, and allowed myself to become captive to all of this. If we don't go there and get to the root of feeling stuck, we won't be free to explore who we want to be. Being who you want to be isn't about changing who you are. It's about tapping into who you are: your strengths, gifts, and talents. You have a bigger purpose, and this world needs you. People need what you have to give! Are you ready to explore who you want to be?

I have a simple task to get you started. Start thinking about three words that you would like to be known for. What are the first three words that pop into your head? There isn't a right or wrong answer when you begin to do this. My words are inspired, confident, and fearless. These words are significant to me. I want to inspire others but also want to be inspired. I want to be confident in who I am because, I had no idea what being confident meant for so long. The word fearless is special to me because I lived in fear of not being good enough for so long. Your words will become significant to you as you begin to explore who you truly desire to be. Words are powerful. These words will become the foundation of your "personal brand." You see, just like companies create a brand to tell a story and to connect with others, you are also your brand. Everything you do can flow from your brand.

Often, we embrace a wrong perception of who we are because of our painful past or how others have labeled us. Exploring who you want to be will help you stop embracing a false identity. Choosing three words seems like a simple thing, but it can be so powerful if you take this seriously. This can help you reflect on what you stand for and will become a powerful tool in guiding you to where you desire to go and who you desire to be. What has happened to you does not determine where you are going, and it also doesn't define who you are. When we start to believe we are what has happened to us or who others have said we are, we begin to believe a lie which becomes a false identity. Choosing three words that are significant to you will also begin to set the foundation for your future goals. When you know what you stand for, you'll know where you're going. Think about the women you admire. Why do you admire them? What about them stands out to you? How do they shine? What qualities do they have? What do they stand for, and what do they reflect? Are they powerful, intelligent, authentic, fierce?

What is it about them that catches your attention? Think about that for a minute. Please write it down in your journal or notebook. More importantly, think about what you stand for and who you want to be? Who would you like to impact, and how would you impact them? I believe you can influence, inspire, and impact others. And I don't just believe you can. I believe you are meant to. Yes, you, *Amiga*, are meant to influence and inspire the next generation of *Mujeres*. It doesn't matter what you have been through or what mistakes you have made. You are capable of leading those around you.

There is a story in the Bible about a young woman named Esther who became queen. She had no parents, just a cousin who was looking out for her. In this story, a prideful man named Haman wants to kill the Jewish people. No one knew Esther was Jewish, and these were *her* people. The short version of this story is Esther speaks up for her people even though it could have cost her life. She saved her people because of her courage and boldness. Esther did not come from wealth. She was just an ordinary girl. However, she did not allow her past to stop her from speaking up for her people. I believe Esther finally realized the power and authority inside of her. Esther saw herself for who she truly was and not who she had been in the past.

Esther understood the power and authority she carried inside. Someone helped her realize what she carried within. This person challenged her to see herself as more. Her cousin Mordecai tells her in Esther 4:14, "And who knows but that you have come to your royal position for such a time as this?" Girl, I don't know about you, but that pumps me up. Even when things look tragic, and we have gone through so much pain and chaos, we can choose to stand up, speak up, and be bold. If you read the rest of the story in the book of Esther, you will see that she indeed saves her people. The whole story is like a real-life *telenovela*. Sometimes life is like a tragic telenovela episode. You wonder, *When will I finally get to the part where life gets less complicated, less painful, and you finally heal?*

I honestly can't answer that question for you, but I can say that tragedy can become triumph. Think about it, what if you are here for such a time as this? What if, because of you, the future generation of *Mujeres* don't have to suffer because you paved the way for them to be strong, powerful, bold, beautiful, and courageous? You can do that, *Amiga*! I believe you are here for such a time as this. It's time to rock that invisible crown because even if you have experienced pain and made mistakes, God sees you for who you could be. Even if others have rejected you and made you feel worthless, girl, you are so worthy. Your time is now. It's time to rise and turn to a new chapter of your life. This chapter has not been written. It's a blank page right now. So, tell me, *what will you write in your chapter?*

You are here for such a time as this.

— Esther 4:14

The Training Ground

When I was healing from what happened to my daughter, I began to see things more clearly. Although I was still devastated and angry, I learned to focus on where God was taking me. After everything my family and I had been through, I still believed there were better things in store for us. I made sure my daughter knew what had been happening to her was never her fault. I made sure to tell her she was not a victim. I told her the opposite. I told her she was a survivor, and her voice was powerful. Her speaking up is what stopped what was happening to her. I wanted her to understand she was not damaged. She was still beautiful, worthy, and loved. I have seen her struggle throughout the years, but I remind her that she is a strong young woman, and I see her and love her. I call her my Warrior Princess because that's who she is to me. She fought for herself every time she went to therapy and didn't want to. She fought for herself every time she was depressed but still got up. She is a fighter and a survivor. I admire my daughter.

As women, we need to speak life into each other, and we need to remind each other of how powerful we are. We have too much competition, tearing each other down, and judging going on between women. Imagine a world where *Mujeres* came together to lift and celebrate each other? Girl, we would be unstoppable!

When we lift each other up and celebrate each other, something powerful happens. I know that as women, we don't always vibe with each other. Sometimes friendships and family members fall away. I know we are not perfect, but if you can lift other *Mujeres* in your own unique way, please do so. This world needs that, and this world also needs your gifts and talents. You never know where you will go once you allow your gifts and talents to shine. Trust me, girl, I've seen it!

If you are reading this book, it might be because you've heard me on *The Fearless Mujer Podcast*. Can I tell you something? I never wanted to start a podcast or coach or any of that. It really wasn't in my plans. I did it because I felt that other women needed to know they were not alone. My first podcast was faith-based, and very early on, women were reaching out to me on Instagram, telling me how encouraged they were by an episode. Some women would share personal and deep stuff with me. I started to mentor women and didn't even realize I was doing it. When a woman would reach out to me, I would ask if they wanted to jump on Zoom and talk. I was healing more just because I made myself available to other women throughout this time. I started to find my voice and began to walk into my authority.

Finding my voice evolved from a place of being uncomfortable. I felt awkward, nervous, and scared at the beginning of my podcast journey. I felt like giving up so many times. I was still fighting through a lot of limiting beliefs about myself. I kept going because if other women were telling me the podcast was helping them, then I couldn't stop no matter how I felt. I began to connect with so many amazing women of all places on Instagram. And my podcast was also growing.

Dear Fearless Mujer, You Were Created for More

I would have never met these women if it wasn't for social media. But then, almost one year into the podcast, I started to feel like I needed to go in a different direction. I felt called to speak specifically to Latina women. One night, I started to pray and dig deep into this new inspiration on my way to therapy. Right there in my Buick, *The Fearless Mujer Podcast* was born! I launched my podcast because, as I look back, I really wish someone would have looked out for me and spoken life into me. I wish there had been someone who would have magnified my gifts and talents. I wish there had been someone to help me become the woman I was meant to be. Today there are so many women struggling with their identity.

Some come from broken homes or do not have resources. Some women have not had it easy and have always figured things out alone. Not all of us came from an ideal environment. Many *Mujeres* had to figure things out on their own and make things happen. That's why I created *The Fearless Mujer Podcast* because we are not meant to stay stuck where we are. We are not meant to hide behind our pain or past mistakes. There is so much more you were created for. Being fearless means you lack fear. When you can step into the fearless part of yourself, you will learn how free and brave you can be. If life has knocked you down and you've been through some crazy stuff and been hurt, you don't have to allow that to hold you back from where you are going in life.

Sometimes things that happen, things people say, or mistakes we make will hold us back from walking in our purpose. Many women live deeply wounded because of their past pain. Sometimes life hardens our hearts, and I can understand why. The painful things, the negativity, the hard things, and the setbacks seem purposeless and impossible to overcome at that moment. But what if those things are what helps you step into your purpose? What if that molds you into the woman you are meant to be so that you can help others? What if all the hard things are what launch you into your purpose? What if you are meant to be a light to others? Sometimes the setbacks, the pain, the trials, and the heartache are your stepping stone to something greater.

Sometimes those things that seem tragic at the time are your training ground for the next chapter of your life. You can choose not to allow your painful past to victimize you. I know it can be easier to say that than to believe it. I thought I would always be a victim to my past, but now I know all my pain was a training ground. At the time, I couldn't see it. I was so devastated and so hurt, but I am so grateful that I held on to my faith and allowed myself to begin healing. My voice became a tool to help other women, and now I know my bigger purpose is to help others.

I know now my past does not define me. I am aware that even if others remember me a certain way or define me based on the season of my life when they knew me, that doesn't mean they know the person I am today. Sometimes we make the mistake of allowing the opinions of others to define who we are. I am not the girl I used to be. You are not the girl you used to be, because your past does not define you. *Amiga*, your identity is not based on what people have said about you. When others try to label you because of your past, please remind yourself that you are not the girl you used to be.

I found my voice while I was literally using my voice. I used my voice in the past to hurt others to protect myself. I found the voice that I once felt didn't matter, so I kept it hidden. I found the voice that the pain, trauma, and dysfunction almost stole from me. I found it, and it freed me because I could finally be myself. There is so much freedom in being yourself.

Amiga, I am an ordinary girl. I don't come from wealth; I don't hold the highest academic credentials. My life could have ended up completely different. I don't even think my life should be where it is today. I'm a Mexican girl who grew up in a broken and dysfunctional home in Little Village, a rough neighborhood on the Southwest side of Chicago. I struggled with my identity growing up and didn't have much guidance. I had kids young, and I was just trying to survive. I didn't have confidence in myself. I was suicidal and felt that my life didn't matter. I had to learn to see myself through new eyes and not through the eyes of others. When I learned to see myself the way God saw me, I understood I truly had a purpose. I also understood I didn't have to apologize or get permission for being who I was created to be.

Despite what others may say, I know I am not the girl I used to be. I am God's daughter and surrendering my life to Jesus is the only way that I found true freedom. I found my life when I surrendered it fourteen years ago. You see, even when this world has tried to break me or life throws painful curve balls at me, I know there is a God who will use it all for something greater.

My favorite Bible verse is Romans 8:28, "And we know that in all things God works for the good of those who love him, who have been called according to his purpose." It reminds me that even during bad times, God is working everything out for my good. God will give you purpose because you are not here by accident. I am not here to shove my beliefs down your throat. I am simply sharing my story, and I can't share it without telling

89

you what God did in my life and how He gave me purpose and true freedom. Whether you believe in God or not, *Mujer*, please know I love you. I see you, and I think you're amazing! I want you to know your voice is powerful, and it matters. You may have already found your voice, or maybe you're still on that journey. You might be wondering what that looks like for you? What does it mean to find your voice? As an empowerment coach and pod-caster, I've had the privilege of meeting many different women. Many have told me they felt like they never had a voice. Others have told me they were told they were *too much*. Could it be possible that some girls were designed to be *too much*? Talk too much, voice their opinions, and speak their mind because they are natural-born leaders?

Look, I don't know what being *too much* means, but I don't think any *Mujer* is ever too much. We are each made in a unique way. I don't believe we should make girls feel bad for being strong and opinionated. Instead, we should teach our daughters, sisters, nieces, etc., how to use their strong voices in a way that will influence those around them. In the past, I used my voice to tear others down because I was constantly in survival mode. I was always trying to protect myself. Growing up in dysfunction teaches you to operate in survival mode, but it does not teach you to use your voice powerfully or wisely. When you finally come to a point in life where you realize that you no longer need to operate in survival mode, you will learn how to tap into the power of your voice.

I believe deep down inside, everyone has a message, and if they were able to tap into that message, this world would be a much better place. This world is such a big place, and what if you could impact others just by using your voice? Even if others have rejected you and made you feel worthless in the past, know that you are worthy and valuable. Girl, your message is powerful, and it truly matters. Your voice can impact so many lives. From the beginning of my podcasting journey, my message to every woman has been, "you are worthy, you were created for a purpose, and your past does not define you." That is still the message in my heart. I rebranded and pivoted my podcast and began to speak to a specific group of women, but the message in my heart didn't change. Developing the message you want to mark the world with is powerful. Despite what your past looks like, it does not disqualify you from sharing your message with the world. So, what does your message look like? What would you like to share with others, and who specifically would you like to share it with? How do your message and voice stand out?

Finding your voice may not look like starting a podcast. It may look very different for you. It could be that you start a book club, a community for women, a blog, or a business. Finding your voice might even look like making jewelry, writing a book, mentoring women, or starting a Bible study if you feel inspired to do that. Whatever it looks like for you, trust it's the right thing for you. Remember finding your voice is a process, be patient with yourself and show yourself grace.

The setback, pain, and trial can be your stepping stone to something greater.

Dear Fearless Mujer, You Were Created for More

Mujer, You Have Authority

When I started my business, *Fearless Mujer, LLC,* and began coaching, I knew I needed to help women work through the limiting beliefs and lies holding them back. I knew it was important, and it was my area of gifting. Becoming a certified coach can teach you the *proper* way to coach, but I also believe that the ability to coach and mentor others is a gift. Coaching is a tool that can help a person succeed as they grow and evolve, and it's also a beautiful gift that can transform a person. I understood a big reason women have a hard time getting to where they want to go are the limiting beliefs that become deeply-rooted lies. Beliefs that become deeply rooted lies will need to be exposed if you plan on stepping into your purpose.

Without exposing those beliefs, we will try everything to get to where we want to go, but it will be hard. Here's the thing, if you don't expose the limiting beliefs you have, it will be hard to see clearly. So, let's get one limiting belief out of the way. This belief tells you that other women are smarter than you. It might whisper to you, "You don't belong here." This belief might make you feel that your life, voice, or story don't matter. This belief will say no one cares about what you have to say. This belief lies and says you don't have a purpose. This is the limiting belief I call *purposeless.* If you have this belief, girl, it's time to destroy it! I am not a limiting belief expert. However, I am a woman who has had to do the painful work of exposing her own false beliefs. I've had to expose the deeply rooted lies I carried. I have also helped women work through their limiting beliefs, and once they do this, they are relieved because they stop feeling like something is wrong with them. It's so refreshing when you get to the place where you realize nothing is wrong with you and that the problem wasn't you, it was the limiting beliefs you had.

The *purposeless* belief is deeply rooted in childhood abuse, trauma, rejection, childhood neglect, and more. I believe this because if at a young age you start to believe you're worthless, garbage, unwanted, unloved, in the way, a punching bag, then you will wonder why you are even here. You start to believe the lie that tells you your life doesn't even matter. *Amiga*, if you have been holding onto this lie, it's time to release it. Do not embrace this lie and do not take ownership of it. This lie was never yours. Please grab a paper and pen right now. If you don't have a paper and pen and are not driving, please text yourself what I am about to say, "I will not take ownership of the lie that tells me I am purposeless. This was never my lie, and I will no longer embrace it and I will release it." Why am I telling you to write this? Because there is power in writing it and seeing the words you have written. You will have to continue exposing this lie because a limiting belief is like a weed. Sometimes it tries to come back.

Now that we have done some heart work, it's time to dive into the truth about who you are. *Mujer*, you are here for a greater reason! Your life is significant. Even if it feels like life has beaten you up, you still have a purpose. So many people go through life searching for their purpose, yet it is already inside them. That's why some people are passionate about art, writing, serving others, etc. Something pulls them to that specific thing. You see this in movies often when a person decides they don't want to go to college anymore because they want to travel the world, help orphans, or start a business. They willingly choose to chase a bigger dream.

Have you ever wondered what causes a person to do that? In a movie they usually devastate a parent who had high expectations for their child going to college or maybe running the family business. But that person still chooses to pursue what they are truly passionate about. I know I described something entirely fictional, but this happens often. If I were to ask you what you would love to do if money and time weren't an issue, what would you say to me? If you knew that you could live the life you desire in the next year, what would that look like for you? What goals do you need to set to pursue this bigger dream?

Sometimes we don't take time to analyze what we truly desire. We neglect the dreams we are still holding onto. Sometimes we start living life on autopilot, and we forget the dreams we once had. I genuinely believe when you understand what fuels you to pursue something, you will set the right goals and begin to see your purpose unfold. This takes time, so don't feel like you have to rush it. In the next chapter, we will dive into your bigger dream, but for now, I want you to think about when you were little. Think about what you loved to do and what made you feel excited. Have you ever watched a child play and use their imagination? They don't have limits to what they want to do. Children are the biggest dreamers. They will tell you that they want to be an astronaut, president, a samurai, or a millionaire. They don't limit what they want to do until someone tells them they can't do that because it's unrealistic. We should tap into our inner child to understand what fills us with passion. You see, I believe your unique experiences growing up can reveal your gifts and your passions.

Think about when you were little, what did you want to do or be? What is something that used to excite you that you stopped wanting? What is something you used to dream about? If you're unsure about your gifts, this can help reveal some of what those are. Let me share a personal example; I loved playing restaurant when I was little. I would pretend I was a waitress and take my dad's order. When I got older, I became a waitress. I didn't always love it, but I felt a sense of joy and satisfaction when someone was happy with my service. I found out I enjoyed serving others because serving is one of my gifts. I genuinely love serving others, but now I don't do it through waiting tables. I do it through coaching and podcasting. Throughout my years working, I would always get asked to train someone or teach someone something specific at work. That still happens to me quite a lot. People ask me to teach them how to do something, whether podcasting or creating engaging content. Teaching is also one of my gifts, and that's exactly what I do when I'm podcasting or coaching. Honestly, I love it so much!

Every single one of my experiences has led me to this point in my life. Of course, back then, I never would have guessed it. I couldn't see that a lot of what I was doing was part of my area of gifting. But slowly, I have been able to connect the dots and discover my gifts. Think back on your life, when you were in school or around friends, what did you enjoy doing? Did you enjoy speaking in front of others? Did you love helping the teacher? Where were you in different scenarios? Think about when you were at home, what were you doing? What can you remember yourself doing? Did anyone ask you to help cook, read, or write something? Were you told you were good at speaking, writing, cooking? What made you excited and happy? Think about your life today. Do you see a theme to what you are passionate about? Exploring this about yourself is crucial because you will have clarity once you understand this about yourself. When you're unsure about what you're passionate about and confused about your gifts, it's easy to start comparing yourself to others. Comparison distracts you from setting goals and pursuing your dreams. If you struggle with comparing yourself to others, please know you're not alone. Many women struggle with this. If you want to stop comparing yourself to others, focus on your gifts and what you are passionate about.

We all have gifts inside of us ready to be unleashed. There are skills you can acquire and knowledge you can gain, but there are also things that you are naturally good at. You might be a great speaker and communicator. Maybe when you are in the room with other people and start to speak, people are intrigued by what you have to say. Have you ever wondered why? There are people gifted in one area, and you can see their gifts shine. The truth is everyone walking this Earth has natural gifts and abilities. If you are thinking right now, *Micaela, that's not me*. I'm not good at anything.

Well, I would like your permission to challenge that thought. You see, once you begin to tap into your area of genius, you will see your gifts flourish. When you tap into your area of genius, you are tapping into your gifts and strengths. When you do this, you get better and stronger, and you become more confident.

Sometimes we believe the lie that says, "Oh, that person is better than me, and I could never do that." I'll admit it. I've done that in the past. Be careful if you have thoughts like that. That's how comparison starts, and it's so easy to get caught in that ugly trap. You'll start to compare what you are doing with what others are doing. Have you ever compared yourself to someone doing something similar to what you are doing? What about when you see another *Mujer* doing something cool or interesting, and you get curious about it? Maybe you even decide you want to try that thing out only to find out what you started doing isn't in your area of genius. Now you have started to do something you don't even enjoy doing, and you force yourself to do it, even though you are not passionate about it. That's why people quit things because they realize they started doing something that wasn't in their area of genius, and they aren't passionate about it. Put it this way, it's like trying to wear a cute pair of shoes that don't fit you, and you get a blister, or your toe starts to hurt bad. That doesn't feel good. Forcing yourself to do something that's not your area of genius because you think it will be cool, or you think you would make a lot of money at it, also doesn't feel good. You are forcing yourself to do something that just doesn't fit.

But, when you step out of your comfort zone and put yourself out there, you will begin to see your natural gifts shine. The more you do what you are gifted at, the better you'll get at what you are doing.

It can be easy to think that a person was born good at something. We might even think they didn't have to put any effort into that specific thing. But that's not always true. Many people have mastered their craft, stepped out of their comfort zone, and focused on where they were gifted. By focusing on their gifts, they became great at what they were doing. When you start doing something you're gifted at, you will grow. When you pursue what you are passionate about and good at, you become more equipped in that area. When you become equipped, you will grow in confidence and begin stepping into your authority. When I say authority, I don't mean you start to boss everyone around or start to walk in arrogance. I mean reclaiming your right to be the woman you were created to be. Despite the hard things you have been through, that doesn't disqualify you from living the life you were meant to live. Stepping into your authority means not allowing yourself to be held back by past pain, mistakes, or what others have said. *Mujer*, you are the only one who knows a lot about your life, your story, and past experiences.

You decide how to share it, when to share it, or who to share that part of yourself with. No one gets to decide that for you. Even if others want to say negative things about certain parts of your life, they still do not have the authority to talk about your life. So many *Mujeres* have made the mistake of allowing others to take ownership of their story or parts of it. Stepping into your authority means taking ownership of your story, your past mistakes, past pain, and even what others have said. When you take ownership of this, you decide if your past mistakes define you, not someone else. You decide if your past pain holds you back. You decide if what others have said about you is relevant or not.

You decide how and when you share your story. All of that belongs to you, and you get to decide if you share it. No one gets to decide that for you! No one gets to dictate these things for you.

This is how you empower yourself and begin to step into your boldness. Just like Queen Esther, who was determined not to allow her people to perish, and because of this, she saved them and stepped into a new boldness. You are the one who chooses not to allow your future self to perish. If you allow your past pain and what others have said to define you, you risk not becoming who you were meant to be. Even if others have rejected you and made you feel like you're nothing special, there is so much more to your life than what you can see on the surface. There is still so much more for you beyond what you could ever imagine.

Mujer, no matter what has happened to you, you are not damaged goods. Your stories, life experiences, and even your mistakes can become your message. Your message can become your superpower! No one can take your message because it's yours. Your stories, even the painful ones, are yours. You have authority over these things, which makes you the expert of your life, not someone else. Therefore, you get to choose if you share your story with others. You are the one who chooses to share your message with the world. I understand your life is not a *telenovela*, and you may not want people to know your business. I completely get that, and I am not telling you to tell everyone your business. But I want to ask you to think about the possibility that your story could help someone else. What if your message was the key to helping someone not have to experience something painful? What if your story could help someone else receive inner healing? Our past pain could be a beautiful treasure for someone else. Your painful story could be another Mujer's beautiful treasure. The story you carry can empower others. We carry stories with us that can offer hope to others. I once heard a pastor say your trauma could be someone else's shortcut. Your story is so powerful it can transform others.

What you have experienced could be the key someone else needs to open a door that might set them free from their pain. If you've experienced domestic violence and you found your way out of it, your story can empower another person to find their way out of it. Your message could literally help so many people. Don't be ashamed of what you have gone through. Some things were beyond your control. If it's a mistake you are holding onto, release it and let go of the shame. Your mistakes can also be a shortcut for someone else. All of that can become a beautiful message. Think about how your story could become a beautiful message? The story that becomes your message can lead you right into your purpose. Maybe you're reading this, and you're like, "Girl, you have no idea what I have been through. My life has been so painful." I get that, and I don't want you to force this because it may not be your time to share that part of your story or message.

Inner healing has to happen before that time comes, and that journey will be painful. That's why it's important to rewrite the lies you believe about yourself and begin to remove the labels that others have placed on you. You cannot allow others to define you or your message. If you are not at the point where you are ready to share your story, know that it's okay. Keep doing the inner heart work and keep affirming yourself. You will know when it's your time to share your beautiful message. You will have peace and will also feel the freedom to do so. Please don't disqualify yourself if you have felt like your story doesn't matter. Each *Mujer* has a beautiful message that this world needs.

Amiga, you have a beautiful message, and even your painful stories can become a beautiful message. Painful stories are not always easy to talk about because sometimes the pain has a way of holding us captive. Pain is a real thing that not many people want to face. It is always easier to bottle it up and pretend it doesn't exist. For some, it's easier to drink the pain away, smoke the pain away, or find another way to numb the pain. At that moment, those options sound good and convenient, but over time those options hold us captive to the pain we have not yet escaped. There is no exit door to the pain. At some point, you will have to come face to face with a part of your story that needs to be dealt with. The bravest thing you could ever do is confront the pain. Don't be ashamed of it. I get that this may not be easy for a lot of people. It has not been easy for me. I was raised to think that if I cried, I was weak. I was taught not to cry, so instead, I ignored the things that hurt me. I became an emotional wreck and roller coaster.

Only by God's grace and my healing journey have I become whole. I know what it feels like to be broken inside because of all the pain. I know the anxiety that comes when you fear you may never be whole. I know the shame that takes over when the pain becomes your comfort zone. Pain has a way of wrapping you up in shame disguised as a security blanket. The shame will isolate you and hold you, prisoner. It will lie to you and tell you if people knew what you've been through, they wouldn't love you. Shame will give you anxiety and make you want to hide from the world. Shame is not your friend because shame will never allow you to shine or blossom into the person you were created to be. Shame will continue to hold you captive to pain because that is where it thrives. Shame is like a parasite controlling your every thought. If you are carrying shame, girl, you have to destroy it. I would suggest working with a therapist who can help you walk through your healing journey because confronting pain is never easy. But once you do, you will be so grateful that you did because then you will begin to see clearer. When we focus on our pain, we become hindered from reaching our full potential.

Amiga, you need to know there is a bigger purpose for your life despite what anyone has said or done to you. I would never have thought that about myself five or ten years ago. I felt that I had no purpose in this life. But I wouldn't be writing this book if it wasn't for all the pain that I have been through. The pain prepared me, and the trauma transformed me. You see, sometimes God will turn your pain into purpose and give you a crown of beauty for your ashes, just like it says in Isaiah 61:3. What was meant to defeat you will instead be what guides you into your purpose. Your pain does not disqualify you from stepping into your God-given purpose. You may feel you don't have a purpose and wonder why you are even here. I used to wonder the same thing for many years. I was suicidal and wondered why I was I born. I felt like my life didn't matter. Even as a woman of faith who is a follower of Jesus, I have endured many hard things. Pain does not discriminate. It doesn't care about your faith, degrees, or how much money you have. Pain is something we all experience. We cannot escape it; we have to face it and overcome it.

Mujer, no matter how painful your life has been, you are still worthy of living out your purpose. There is so much goodness inside of you, even if others have told you otherwise. Even if others tore you down with their words your whole life, that doesn't erase your purpose. Even when those who were supposed to love and protect you didn't, it still doesn't erase your purpose. When those you loved have betrayed you, that still doesn't erase your purpose. *Amiga*, you have a beautiful purpose and so much to live for. Don't forget that.

> Your painful story can be another *Mujer's* beautiful treasure.

Dear Fearless Mujer, You Were Created for More

Girl, Stop Escaping Reality

I used to think dreams only came true for special people. I believed the *it's not for me* lie, and anytime I saw someone fulfill a dream, that lie slapped me in the face. When you experience many different setbacks in life, you start expecting the worst. If you have been conditioned to believe dreams come true, just not for you, it's time to challenge that belief. The truth is dreams come true if you are willing to work hard to get there. If you're distracting yourself with *telenovelas* and TV shows, it's going to be hard to get to where you're going. I'm serious, *Chica*. You can't accomplish your goals and dreams if you constantly escape reality. Now, don't get me wrong, I also enjoy watching movies and TV shows, so please believe me when I say I am not judging you. A funny movie playing in the background while I cook or clean somehow makes time go by faster.

I also know if all I do is get lost in some *telenovela*, I'll never accomplish important things. I know this because I was the girl sitting in front of the TV for hours and hours, letting my day pass me by because I was battling anxiety and depression. I didn't feel like I was good enough, so I allowed myself to get lost in a fictional character. When this fictional character achieved what they wanted, I was still in the same place I was when the movie or TV show started. Look, *Amiga*, I love you, and that's why I'm going there. If you plan to get serious about where your life is going, then it's time to pay attention to some of the things you are doing. It's time to turn off the TV and start developing your gifts and talents. I'm not saying you shouldn't watch *telenovelas* or movies.

What I'm saying is don't distract yourself because you're too afraid of becoming the woman you were meant to be. The beauty of this life is that we can choose where we go beyond where we are now. Are you willing to forsake your comfort zone to pursue your bigger dream? How bad do you want the dream in your heart? Even if others have doubted you or you have doubted yourself, it's not too late for you to start pursuing the bigger things in your heart. If I can be honest, not everyone will be happy when you choose to pursue something entirely out of the box. Not everyone will get your big dream or what you are trying to accomplish, but *guess what?* This book is not about them. It is about giving yourself permission to be who you were created to be. Even if you don't feel super confident about pursuing your dreams at this very moment, that's okay. You don't need to be the most confident to start. You just need to be who you are. Authenticity is key to pursuing your bigger dream.

You won't ever hear me say, "Girl, fake it 'til you make it." I don't believe in that, and I'm sure some might give a reason why it's a good idea, but I never tell my clients or listeners that out of my own conviction. I'm not a "fake it 'til you make it" kind of girl. I'm more of the show up authentically until you make it type of girl. Then when you make it, keep showing up authentically. "Fake it 'til you make it" is a lie. Why would you want to be someone other than who you are? It's like putting a band-aid on a deeper issue.

What if the reason you are "faking it 'til you make it" is because you're scared? Wouldn't it make more sense to work through the fear rather than fake it? You see, becoming the woman you were created to be isn't about making everyone like you or having a bunch of followers. The truth is, not everyone will like what you have to say, write, or even the story you want to share. But that's okay. That's how you weed out the people who aren't really there for you and make space for those who will genuinely love and believe in you. Some people are only meant to be in your life for a season, including family. But never think that you can do it alone. You will always need someone to bounce ideas off of, and you will always need someone to encourage you to set goals that lead you to pursue your dream. In the eighth chapter, I'll tell you what I've learned from having mentors and why I believe they are needed. But for now, let's dive into your passions.

If I were to ask you what you're passionate about, what would you say to me? Think about it for a minute. *What are you passionate about?* What does it mean to be passionate about something? Passion can drive you to do things that you never thought possible. You might already know what you are passionate about. You might be scared or worried about what will happen if you start pursuing what you're passionate about? If you don't know what you're passionate about, that's okay. You just need to explore this more to have clarity. So, let me ask you this, what lights you up? What can you talk about for hours that excites you and brings you joy? What upsets you? Paying attention to what brings you joy and what upsets you can reveal a lot about what you are passionate about. Start to observe these things about yourself.

Think about people who pursue social justice. They do this because they are passionate about seeing justice happen. Other people might be passionate about seeing hungry children have the food they need so that they don't ever go hungry again. Someone passionate about helping hungry children might create a nonprofit to help kids or collaborate with an organization that's already doing this. Pay attention to everything about who you are and what fills your heart with passion. Is there something constantly tugging at your heart? You might dream about it, and maybe you can picture yourself there. So, what is it that tugs at your heart, and no matter how much you try, it won't go away? It's almost like you can't seem to shut it off. If you have no idea what fills your heart with passion, then you will need to dig even deeper into this part of yourself. You have to get to know who you are and what you want without the titles you carry, what you do daily, or the negative things people have said about you. You have to dig deep if you genuinely plan on discovering what you are passionate about.

Imagine you didn't have anything or anyone standing in your way. Where would you want to be next year? What would you want to be doing? Get creative and use your imagination. Whatever fills your heart with passion is worth exploring. If something fills your heart with passion, no matter how crazy you think it sounds, chances are you may want to take a closer look. What you are passionate about can reveal more about what you are meant to do. Your passion can connect you to your bigger dream, and your passion will reveal the bigger *why* to you.

Many women have dreams and aspirations, but without a big enough reason or bigger *why*, they will fail to set the appropriate goals for the vision for their life. It's important to understand your reasons for wanting to pursue your dreams. Your dreams are so important, and they matter. Your dreams can help others, and truly influence and impact the next generation of women.

Dreaming isn't just for some people. Dreaming is part of our purpose. The things that we feel passionate about are there for a reason. You are meant to pursue that thing in your heart. That's why it's there. You might be able to envision what that thing is for you, and if you can't envision it right now, you will in time if you stay focused and intentional. Maybe because of circumstances, you have let go of what you were once passionate about. Maybe someone discouraged you or mocked your idea, or you feel like it's too late for you.

Girl, it is never too late to pursue those big things. If you have no idea what that looks like for you, please take your time exploring this. Now, let's dig into what you are passionate about. Let's do some brainstorming together. What fills you with joy when you are doing that thing at that moment? What have you previously said you love to do? Do you love to serve and to help others? Does it make you happy when you help a specific group of people? Do you have a burden to help the homeless? Do you desire to help and serve single moms? What if you are meant to create an organization that helps homeless people or single moms? Do you love to make clothes or jewelry because that's how you help women feel beautiful? What if you are meant to have a jewelry or clothing business? Brainstorming with questions like this will help you gain clarity. Your answers to these questions will be different from anyone else's. And even if it looks similar, that's okay. The thing you are meant to do won't be like someone else's because you are unique. Your dreams and goals are unique to who you are, and no one can replicate what you are meant to do.

Even if others don't understand your dream or why you want to pursue whatever that is for you, don't stop. Don't stop before you start. You don't have to give everyone access to the dreams in your heart. Have you ever shared your dreams with someone, and they tried to discourage you from pursuing that dream? Maybe it was a family member who gave you every reason why the thing you wanted to do wouldn't work or why you would fail if you pursued it? Here is a truth bomb for you: some people won't believe in your dream. Some people will not believe in your big dream because they can't believe in their own big dream. Big dreams scare people sometimes. It's the fear of the unknown. It's the question everyone wonders, *What if I don't make it?* Have you ever asked yourself that? I used to ask myself that question, but all it does is instill doubt in yourself. Now I ask myself, "What if I do make it?" *Mujer*, you cannot allow others to take ownership of your dream. Not everyone needs access to your dreams. Your dreams are yours to pursue. We give people access to our dreams sometimes without even realizing it.

Have you ever heard the story of Joseph in the Bible? He had extraordinary dreams God gave him, but he shared his dreams with his brothers because he was young and naive. His brothers already didn't like him because he was his father's favorite. They hated him so much they sold him into slavery. Those who were supposed to love Joseph ended up being the ones who betrayed him. That didn't stop Joseph from being who he was meant to be. God used Joseph's literal dreams to position him. Joseph became a very influential man who impacted others and helped others, including those who betrayed him. You can read this story if you like in Genesis 37.

Sometimes others won't feel happy about your dream. They will look at you like you're crazy for even thinking about doing that thing. Sometimes people will also continue to see you as the girl who messed up. To some people, you may always be the girl who got pregnant young, the woman who got divorced, the girl who dropped out of school, the woman who lost her temper that one time, the girl who ran with the wrong crowd, you can fill in the blank. But we have all made mistakes and had horrible chapters in our life. No one is excluded from that. Even if to some you'll always be the girl who messed up, to God, you'll always be the one He can use to accomplish His purpose in you and through you. If you have been disqualifying yourself because of your past, don't do it anymore. If you feel like your life was meant for more, it's because it is. Write this down, "I am not letting others influence my dreams anymore." Put it where you can see it to remind yourself that your dreams are valuable. Your dreams are so valuable they can influence future generations.

Now let's dive deeper. How will *you* begin to pursue your dreams? As you explore what you're passionate about and dive into discovering your bigger dreams, it's extremely important to begin exploring your *why*. Getting clear on your *why* will be a powerful tool to help you set the right goals to fulfill the dreams in your heart and the *bigger* dream. Your *why* is all about understanding your reasons for wanting to pursue your dreams. If you don't have clarity on this, you will be all over the place, and it can become easy to start projects that you never finish. Knowing your *why* is crucial. Your *why* will be the heartbeat of why you are doing what you are doing. Your *why* will be key to setting the right goals for you that will lead you to pursue your bigger dream. It will also be what brings longevity to your goals. Pursuing your dream will require you to stick to your goals. This will require you to commit to your goals, step out of your comfort zone, be flexible, and give yourself grace as you begin this journey.

Let's go back to the idea of starting a jewelry business, so I can give you an example of why being clear on your *why* is important. You genuinely love to help women feel beautiful, so you decide to start a jewelry business. You start setting your goals for this, you get focused, and you're super pumped. But then your *Tia* Nancy, who happens to be a negative Nancy, gives you a million reasons why your idea won't work and why your business will fail. She tells you there's too much competition, your jewelry is overpriced, it's a waste of time, and you should just be happy with your job. You get discouraged and sad because you know there is so much more for you, and you see the bigger vision for your business. *Tia* Nancy means well, and maybe she thinks she is helping you. She might have good intentions, but she doesn't see your bigger vision. She doesn't know your *why* behind what you are doing. Knowing your *why* is going to be the fuel that keeps you going. Your *why* is crucial to committing to your goals and to pursuing your bigger dream. Explore your *why* by asking the following questions:

- Why do I want to start _____
  (fill in the blank)?
- Is this idea something that I can't ignore?
- Does my idea or thing in my heart help
  others?
- Will this idea or thing in my heart leave a
  long-lasting impact?
- What is one small thing I can start doing that
  will lead me to accomplish this dream?

Make a list of three short-term goals that you want to accomplish within the next thirty to sixty days and ask yourself, what is within your control that you can start doing now? For example, if you want to go back to school, start researching schools. If your goal is to start a clothing business, maybe you can start talking to people who already have one. This is all about taking baby steps or, as I call it, setting up baby goals to get there.

Asking these questions is going to help you get focused on your goals. It will also help you pursue your goals and dreams with confidence.

As you begin to pursue your dreams, *always* believe that you can do it! You have to believe in yourself so much that what others might say about your dreams and goals will not bother you. Believe you can pursue your dreams. You have to be your biggest cheerleader, even when you feel alone on this journey. Please know I am cheering for you! Don't let anything stop you. You got this, *Mujer*. I believe in you!

Dreaming isn't just for some people. Dreaming
is part of our purpose.

Amiga, You Have a Bigger Purpose

So much of what I have shared with you was not easy. Sharing with you that my daughter was sexually abused was not easy. I mean, who wants to talk about their child experiencing sexual abuse? Sharing with you that my father turned his back on me was also not easy. I don't think anyone would really like to focus on talking about the betrayal of a loved one. No one does. I sure didn't, but if this book can help just one woman believe in herself and reclaim her confidence, then it was worth it. If this book helps one woman who has been imprisoned by a painful secret finally find the strength to release that secret, then it is worth it. If this book helps one *Mujer* feel seen and heard, it was also worth it.

Whatever you have been through, I want you to know that I see you. You didn't come to this book by accident. Maybe you personally know me, and I gifted this book to you. Maybe you heard about it on the podcast, and you couldn't wait to read it. Maybe someone gave you this book. However you got it, I am so grateful you read it. If this book helped you in any way, please pass it along to another fearless *Mujer*.

There is so much power when we lift each other up. Each of us has a story, and no one is more important than the other. We each have been hurt, but we can help each other heal. I want to give a special thank you to the *Mujeres* who read this book and don't believe in God or scripture. Thank you for giving me a safe place to share part of my story. You are amazing! *Amiga*, I want you to know you are safe here. Your story matters, and you never have to be ashamed of what you have been through. I know the pain of never feeling safe. I know the anxiety that comes with shame. I know the pain of being talked about and judged for my past mistakes. I know the lie that says no one really loves me or likes me. I know the pain of feeling unloved and unwanted. I also know the pain of being betrayed and rejected by someone who was supposed to love and protect me. I know what it's like to cry myself to sleep because the past keeps coming back to haunt me. I also know the freedom of letting go. I know the joy that comes when you realize what once hurt you doesn't anymore. I also know the peace of forgiving those who have betrayed me.

Amiga, I want you to know that *your* story is beautiful. Your story is significant, and even if others have hurt you, you matter. My story isn't over, and neither is yours. We are constantly growing, evolving as women, and discovering new things about who we are. It's like a staircase, there is always another step to get to, and each step is a new milestone. Some milestones aren't material things. Some milestones are forgiveness, love, confidence, freedom, and not all milestones look the same for everyone. Whatever milestone you're on your way to accomplishing, please give yourself grace. Sometimes we set high expectations for ourselves and put extra pressure on ourselves. I'm not saying not to set expectations for yourself. We should have some standards and expectations for whatever we accomplish. But I believe some things happen in seasons. Just like the weather changes and we experience different seasons, we also experience different seasons in our lives. In one season, it may feel sunny. In another, it may often be raining, or maybe everything feels cold and silent. In another season, you may finally see things begin to grow. Don't force something to happen that is not meant for that season. Your growth season might look different from someone else's. Your healing season may take longer than someone else's. Whatever your season looks like right now, don't rush anything. Take time to heal, grow, learn new things, and find a mentor. They are so important, and you can't do everything by yourself.

As self-sufficient as I have always been, I had to learn that I couldn't do everything by myself. If I wanted to grow, I would have to surround myself with others who could impart wisdom. It took some time for me to get to where I was ready to hire a mentor and coach. Honestly, it was terrifying at first. You're letting someone in and trusting them, and that takes a lot of courage. I had trust issues, so it was a massive step of faith! You see, I used to think a coach just wanted my money or judged me for needing help. What I have realized is people don't always want your money. Some people really care and want to help you get to where you are going. If you are going to elevate, gain more knowledge, and tap into your strengths and gifts, you will have to say bye to self-sufficiency. You can't do everything yourself because you are not a superwoman. Not everyone will judge you because there will always be someone who has been in your shoes.

Self-sufficiency is an ugly trap that makes you think you don't need anyone to help you.

You may have learned you couldn't depend on anyone, and self-sufficiency became a way to protect yourself. But it's time to stop wearing self-sufficiency like a crown. Please don't believe the lie that you have to be self-sufficient. You don't have to be self-sufficient anymore.

I'm so grateful for the coaches and mentors who believed in me. I wouldn't be here without them. I'm so grateful for the mentors I allowed into my life to help me grow and that I invested in myself. You see, you can want to grow and pursue a dream, but if you don't put some skin in the game, you may not get to where you want to go. When you are invested in what you are doing, you begin to walk the talk because now it's costing you something. I have met many coaches. A lot of them are my friends, and I can tell you they have worked hard to get to where they are and continue to do whatever it takes to get to where they are going. Most of them genuinely have the heart to serve others. If you desire to grow, you must allow someone to speak into you and come alongside you to help you.

There will always be someone who will see something in you that you may not see in yourself. The best thing about a coach/mentor is they believe in you when you don't believe in yourself. They help you connect the dots when you don't understand. Most importantly, they give you the accountability you need. Mentors are everywhere. You just have to find the one who's right for you. Find the one who cares about you and where you are trying to go. A mentor could be someone at the church you go to, a co-worker, or a coach. A coach has already been where you are and understands what it takes to get to where you want to go.

I am so grateful for the coaches who believed in me. I wouldn't be here without their help. I want to thank Stefanie Gass who hosts *The Stefanie Gass Show*. I am so grateful for her heart to teach women how to use their voice and gifts through podcasting. I'm so grateful I could be part of her mastermind because she encouraged me to rebrand and focus on *The Fearless Mujer Podcast*. I am also grateful for Anita Albert-Watson, who created a business program called *Blessed and In Business*. I can honestly say it was what I needed for the beginning of my twelve months in business. Her program set the foundation for my business. I'm so grateful she said yes to the bigger vision God put on her heart. Let me be honest with you, investing in these coaches was a huge step of faith. I didn't have thousands of dollars under my mattress, but I believed God would water the seeds I planted in my business. He did just that. I made more than my investment back.

Next time you think about investing in something, instead of thinking about why it costs so much, think about what you will gain from it and how it will grow you? Look, *Amiga*, I get that sometimes investing on the spot can be challenging, and it may not be the right time. But that shouldn't stop you, because you can start where you are. Start with free resources, books, affordable courses, and work your way up. I believe in the work of a coach when they genuinely have the heart to serve you. When you are ready to find a coach/mentor, make sure their values align with yours, they genuinely want to see you win and believe in you. I would also suggest looking into what others are saying about them. Believe me, when a coach or mentor helps someone, that person will tell others. I pray you will align with those who will help you get where you are meant to go. I also pray you will find a mentor or coach who will celebrate you and your accomplishments. I want to thank my current business coach Whitney Barbary for teaching me it is not arrogant to celebrate myself. I found so much freedom once I understood that. She has been a blessing in my business.

I know there is still so much for me to learn, do, and see, and I am excited to see where my path takes me. The most valuable thing I can say to you is to love yourself and trust yourself. *Love yourself even if others have failed to love you.* Love yourself so that you can heal and grow. When you love yourself and appreciate yourself, you show up differently. You don't show up out of pride or arrogance. You will show up with gratitude and humility. Being humble and grateful will connect you with the right people, those who will genuinely cheer for you. Whatever your journey looks like, you need others to cheer for you. You need others who you can trust.

I never thought I would say that, especially in a book, because I had severe trust issues! If you struggle with trust, take baby steps. I am so grateful to the many women I've crossed paths with. I want to give a special shout-out to the women who have taken time to pour wisdom into me or give me an idea for something that I was working on behind the scenes of my business. Thank you to the *Mujeres* who have believed in me. Not trusting others will hold you back from the path you are meant to be on. It wasn't just people I didn't trust. I didn't trust myself, and I didn't believe in myself. Not trusting yourself will cause you to doubt yourself, and when you doubt yourself, you won't believe in yourself. It's time to trust yourself. Trust that there is more for your life, and you were created for a bigger purpose. Trust yourself and know you can step into your God-given purpose. *Amiga*, I believe in you, and you also have to believe in yourself.

The last thing I want to say is, write yourself a love letter when you have some time. I know it sounds weird and cheesy, but it's a beautiful thing to do for yourself. I've had my past clients do this at the end of their coaching with me, and it's powerful! Write a letter to yourself and include three to five positive qualities about yourself. You're intelligent, inspiring, courageous, beautiful, and powerful. There is no right or wrong way to do this. You can also list your truths and affirmations from the second chapter in this letter.

Finally, write down two or three life experiences that, perhaps, looked like setbacks at the time, but you overcame. In this letter, make a promise to yourself that you will pursue the things in your heart, that you will take time to explore what this looks like for you, and give yourself grace through each step you take to get there. This love letter will motivate you as you enter the next chapter of your life and help you in moments of discouragement. If you would like to share your letter with me, please feel free to do so. I would be honored to read it. You can send your letter to www.fearlessmujer.com/contact, and you can also find me on Instagram at *The Fearless Mujer Podcast*. I love you, *Mujer*, I believe in you, and I am grateful for you. Thank you for trusting me.

God bless you.

Love yourself even if others have failed to love you.

Dear Fearless Mujer, You Were Created for More

Epilogue

I seriously never thought I would have written a book, especially one as deep and personal as this one. If you knew what I've been through, where I come from, and the mistakes I've made, you would say that the odds were against me. I shouldn't be here. As a follower of Jesus, I believe there is spiritual warfare, things unseen to the natural eye. I believe there has been an attack on my life ever since I was a little girl.

When I was five years old, I ran to my parents' garage and into the alley and got hit by a station wagon. It dragged me a few garages down. My mom took me to the emergency room, and would you believe I had no fractures or broken bones? I know, right? It's a *crazy* story.

When I was fifteen, I tried committing suicide by swallowing two bottles of pain medication. But I didn't die. After a few hours, my stomach became nauseated, and I began to throw up every single pill I swallowed. I believe that God's hand was on my life at that moment.

I struggled with depression for many years, and I am so grateful God has freed me from it. In my early twenties, I was a big party girl. I just wanted to numb my pain and fill the emptiness inside me. But nothing seemed to work.

I can honestly tell you if it weren't for my son Fabian, I would have taken my life. He gave me hope to keep holding on.

But it wasn't until I gave my life to Jesus that I could stop numbing the pain. He freed me from the destructive path I was on. I didn't even belong to a church, and trust me, I wanted nothing to do with so-called religion. Accepting Jesus into my heart and life had nothing to do with religion and everything to do with love. I heard of a man who knew my whole life and still loved me. He saw me for who I could be one day and not for who I was in that moment.

I feel like I was just like the woman at the well. If you have never read the story of the Samaritan woman, I suggest you check it out. It's in John 4:7–29. This woman did not have a squeaky-clean background, and as a Samaritan, she wasn't liked by the Jewish people. I assume she jumped from relationship to relationship because when she told Jesus she had no husband, He said, you're right, you've had five! Talk about *keeping it real.* Jesus met her at the well where she went to get water, and He didn't care who she was or what her mistakes looked like. He didn't label her, and the fact that He spoke to her although He was Jewish and she was a Samaritan shows how much He truly loved her and didn't care about labels. That is the Jesus I know. The one who loves, offers mercy, teaches forgiveness, and sticks closer than a brother.

No matter what anyone might say about Jesus, I know He changed my whole life. I have no logical explanation for why my life isn't messed up anymore other than to say, *Jesus changed my whole life.* And after fourteen years of walking with Jesus I am so grateful He has been with me even through the storms.

But I never push my beliefs onto others. I was the girl who didn't want to be preached at. I didn't want to be judged, and I didn't want others to try to fix me. I know that when the time is right, God reaches to the innermost part of His daughters.

I know it takes so much to believe in something you can't see. But that's exactly what faith is. Faith is trusting in what you can't see. Hebrews 11:1 says, "Now faith is confidence in what we hope for and assurance about what we do not see." Faith is something beautiful, and will keep you holding on in the darkest moments of your life.

Why am I sharing this with you? Because like I mentioned before, I probably shouldn't be here today. As I mentioned in this book, if you don't believe in God, I respect that. However, if you are ready to talk more about God and how to start a relationship with Him, girl, I'm here for it. I would be honored to dive into that conversation with you. Please feel free to reach out to me using the links in the appendix.

More than anything, I hope you know your story is not over. There is a much bigger purpose for your life, and if you're a mom, I know how much you desire to be an example to them. As moms, we make so many mistakes but knowing our mistakes can teach our children to be better. As mothers, we have the privilege of influencing our children. Don't believe the lie that says you can't follow your dreams just because you're a mom. You are teaching your kids what's possible when you do.

I pray that this book inspires all three of my children to follow their big dreams and to find a greater purpose in this world.

I believe in you, *Mujer.* May you find your purpose in this world.

Love, Micaela ♡

Endnotes

1   Maya Angelou. Interview with Marianna Schnall. *Psychology Today*. February 17, 2009.

2   Maya Angelou, *I Know Why the Caged Bird Sings*. (New York: Random House, 1979).

3   Bruce Lee, *Striking Thoughts: Bruce Lee's Wisdom for Daily Living*. (Clarendon, Vermont: Tuttle, 2015).

About the Author

Micaela Deegan is a woman of faith, wife, mother, writer, empowerment coach, and podcaster. She is the creator and host of *The Fearless Mujer Podcast* and founded *Fearless Mujer LLC*. Through coaching, she empowers Latina women to become equipped to pursue the bigger dreams in their hearts. She helps them believe in themselves and grow in confidence by giving them tools to identify beliefs that may be holding them back from pursuing their life's purpose. She also hosts monthly *Cafecito + Amigas* Virtual Nights (Coffee + Girlfriend Nights) to offer women community and empowering conversations.

Micaela's passion for helping women comes from years of pain and setbacks. As a young girl who grew up in a rough neighborhood on the Southwest Side of Chicago in a broken and dysfunctional home, she knows firsthand the damage this can do to a young woman. That's why her life's mission is to see women break free from self-limiting beliefs and generational beliefs that hold them back from stepping into their God-given purpose.

Micaela also loves to study God's word, something she grew to love as a student at Liberty University School of Business. When she isn't coaching or podcasting, you can find her hanging out with her family or watching a Hallmark movie.

Appendix

STAY IN TOUCH WITH MICAELA

- Join *The Fearless Mujer* Podcast Community: www.facebook.com/groups/thefearlessmujer
- Grab *The Fearless Mujer Empowerment Guide*: www.fearlessmujer.com/resources
- Keep in touch or sign up for the next *Cafecito + Amiga*s Virtual Event: www.fearlessmujer.com/lets-keep-in-touch
- Stay up to date on Instagram: www.instagram.com/thefearlessmujerpodcast
- Contact to send letters: www.fearlessmujer.com/contact

CPSIA information can be obtained
at www.ICGtesting.com
Printed in the USA
BVHW052340050622
638701BV00005B/20